From Main Street to Wall Street

Making Money in Real Estate

Frank Cappiello

Karel McClellan

John Wiley & Sons

New York • Chichester • Brisbane • Toronto • Singapore

Library of Congress Cataloging in Publication Data:
Cappiello, Frank
    From Main Street to Wall Street: Making money in real estate / Frank Cappiello &
    Karel McClellan

        p.   cm.
        Bibliography: p.
        ISBN 0-471-60067-9
    1. Mortgages—United States.   2. Real estate investment trusts—United States.
    3. Wall Street.   I. McClellan, Karel.   II. Title.
    HB5095.C36 1988   87-33284
    332.63'24—dc19   CIP

Printed in the United States of America

10 9 8 7 6 5 4 3 2 1

Foreword

John M. Templeton

Frank Cappiello and Karel McClellan have provided a book that will help investors learn how to invest and build profits in real estate.

Long before the human race began, animals and birds were claiming ownership of real estate. Observers notice how each pair of mockingbirds claims ownership of a territory and attacks fiercely any other mockingbird entering that area. Much in the Bible concerns the ownership of real estate. The first chapter of *Genesis* records that God said to Adam and Eve, "Multiply and fill the earth and subdue it."

The history books are filled with stories of wars over the ownership of real estate. Real estate was the major form of wealth for thousands of years before stocks and bonds were invented. The value of real estate has always been vastly greater than the value of gold and all other material assets combined. Real estate value continues to increase because man is putting millions more people on earth every month, but God is not creating any more acreage. Throughout history real estate has provided better protection against inflation than has gold or other forms of wealth.

The wealthiest person on earth is the Sultan of Brunei, whose wealth is based on real estate and the oil and gas discovered on his real estate. The wealthiest person in the United Kingdom is the Duke of Westminster; his wealth accrued largely because his ancestors owned a meadow on the edge of the city of London. *Forbes* magazine each year publishes a list of the 400 wealthiest Americans; its latest list contains 73 persons whose wealth derives from real estate.

The market value of all real estate in Japan has more than tripled just in the last three years and reached values never dreamed of before anywhere. The acreage of Japan is less than the acreage of Montana, but official estimates place the value in excess of 150 percent of all real estate of all types in all 50 states of the United States. Recently an estimate was published that the approximate one square mile occupied by the Emperor's Palace in Tokyo has a land value as great as all 159,000 square miles in the state of California.

More than any other asset, the value of a parcel of real estate depends upon location. An acre in the best location may be valued a billion times as high as an acre in the worst location. An acre of land cannot be transported as can other assets, and its value always has and still does depend heavily on politics. This truth was brought home to owners of vast plantations in Cuba when Fidel Castro declared himself a Communist. Even in free enterprise nations, values can be almost totally destroyed by political actions such as rent control or zoning. Growing numbers of nations and states are now imposing restrictions and penalties on the ownership of real estate by foreigners within their borders. It is almost as difficult for a foreigner to buy an acre in Switzerland as in China.

Certain wise investors are always looking for changes in neighborhoods. For example, real estate can increase greatly in value if it is near a major airport or an intersection of interstate highways. Some investors seek real estate that includes water frontage or is suitable for recreation or the building of country homes by city dwellers. The increasing amount of leisure time and upswing in travel result in rapid increases in real estate prices in such areas.

In recent years investors have been offered opportunities to avoid the problem of location by investing in new diversified forms of real estate ownership such as real estate investment trusts, partnerships, development companies, and mutual funds.

The profession of real estate management for absentee owners is growing rapidly. Increasingly it makes sense for investors to diversify their assets by investing in securities based on widespread real estate ownership. American pension funds have now invested more than $150 billion in real estate, which amounts to 7 percent of their total assets. This trend has led to more research and knowledge about ways to invest in real estate. Some professional real estate managers now help investors select wisely on a worldwide scale. They also can help relieve owners of the burdens of tenant problems, repairs, and changing politics.

Investors should always remember that in each location prices of real estate are subject to severe cycles. Each type of property in each area is itself subject to great changes in prices on a cyclical basis. For example, it was quite true that land in south Florida had a great future, but this did not prevent prices from collapsing to one tenth of their highest values or less in some south Florida areas about 60 years ago. Similar cycles will continue in every area and every type of property. Construction of buildings tends to be concentrated at the worst times. Consequently there are alternating periods of surpluses and shortages in each kind of property in each individual area. One way to tell whether prices are dangerously high is when buildings do not consistently sell much higher than the cost of rebuilding that structure in the same area.

Wise investors in real estate should always be prepared to live through a bear market. In other words, it is dangerous to rely on borrowed money.

Successful investing in stocks and bonds requires much more diligence and study than most people think. This is equally true for investors contemplating a portfolio of real estate ownership. That is why this new book by Frank Cappiello and Karel McClellan is essential to you in learning to be a wise and prudent investor.

JOHN M. TEMPLETON
Nassau, Bahamas   Founder and Principal
January, 1988   The Templeton Funds

Preface

The high price of buying real estate on Main Street is bringing more investors to Wall Street—where anyone with a small nest egg can buy quality real estate. Wall Street offers many benefits to real estate investors, among them regular quarterly dividends, strong appreciation potential, a hedge against inflation, a liquid asset, and an investment that requires little management time and attention from the investor.

Historically, real estate has always been a top performer—on Main Street *and* on Wall Street. Today it continues to prove its mettle as a value-oriented, hard asset investment. During 1987's "Black Monday" market slide, real estate stocks demonstrated why prudent investors should always own a healthy ratio of income-producing hard asset-based securities.

From October 1 to October 23, 1987, real estate investment trusts (REITs) dipped only 11 percent, on average, compared with the Dow Jones Industrial Average's 24.9 percent decline and the Standard & Poor's 22.9 percent drop. Real estate investment trusts held their value by a 50-plus percent margin.

This book will show you how to pick real estate winners on Wall Street. It will show you how to select value-oriented stocks with the objective of maximizing your total return through a balanced combination of dividends and capital appreciation.

Whether you're investing for current income, retirement income, or the challenge of the game, this book will give you easy-to-understand guidelines and rules for selecting real estate stocks that meet your specific investment goals.

Equally important, it will give you a sound psychological and analytical foundation for approaching real estate stocks or any other stocks you may be considering. In addition, the Appendix is a fact-filled compendium of investment terminology plus names and addresses useful to any investor looking for real estate investments on Wall Street.

You may be wondering, "Is this a good time to buy real estate or any other stocks?" Now is the best time to buy *if* you know how to locate the best values. This could be your golden opportunity to buy low and, eventually, sell high.

Just four days after Black Monday, 1987, John Templeton, the legendary Wall Street investor, appeared on the award-winning television show, "Wall $treet Week With Louis Rukeyser." Rukeyser asked Templeton, "What's your advice to people in terms of the stock market now?"

Templeton counseled, "Patience. Be a long-term investor. Be prepared financially and psychologically to live through a series of bull markets and bear markets because, in the long run, common stocks will pay off enormously. The next bull market will carry prices far higher than this one . . . because the whole nation is growing more rapidly. The gross national product of the nation will double, at least, in the next 10 years."

On those words of wisdom, we invite you to take a closer look at real estate and Wall Street with us and see how a carefully planned investment program can put steady profits into your portfolio.

And now, welcome to Wall Street.

Baltimore, MD   FRANK CAPPIELLO
Washington, DC   KAREL McCLELLAN
March, 1988

Acknowledgments

The authors wish to express their deep appreciation to those members of the real estate securities industry who took time from their own rigorous schedules to answer technical questions and read draft manuscripts.

We extend our most sincere thanks, in alphabetical order, to: O.R. Bengor, Alex Brown & Sons, Inc.; Donald A. Brown, JBG Associates, Inc.; William N. Cafritz, Trustee, Washington Real Estate Investment Trust; Kenneth Campbell, Audit Investments, Inc.; Robert Frank, Alex Brown & Sons, Inc.; Anne E. Mengdon, Salomon Brothers Inc.; and Fuhrman Nettles, Robert A. Stanger & Company, L.P.

In addition, the authors extend their special thanks to their word-processing staff for dealing so effectively with difficult deadlines, impossible handwriting, and two prima donnas. In alphabetical order, we salute Jane and Joan Anglin, Sharon Silvestri, and Patricia Smith.

Contents

1

Real Estate's Winning Ways

If you think tax reform took the bloom off real estate investment, we have good news for you. Real estate continues to be the top investment choice for long-term, total return. Investor demand remains strong. Institutions, pension funds, foreigners, private developers, wealthy individuals, and small investors are aggressively buying quality real estate for current income and growth potential.

Why is smart money buying real estate today? Because tax reform did not eliminate the traditional benefits of investing in real estate. Investors still enjoy cash flow, growing equity, a strong inflation hedge, and capital appreciation.

Why are knowledgeable investors choosing real estate today? According to Benjamin Holloway, chairman of the Equitable Life Assurance Society's $9-billion real estate portfolio, "Over the long haul, real estate outperforms everything." Holloway recommends putting more than 50 percent of your assets in real estate.

Holloway and Equitable aren't the only professionals banking on the future of real estate. Although Wall Street investment sage Warren Buffet made headlines when he bought 19 percent of the Capital Cities/ABC merger, his purchase of 49.71 percent of the

National Housing Partnership (NHP) received little play by the press. Perhaps the media didn't highlight Buffet's $36-million investment in NHP because the privately held company is not well known on Wall Street and lacks the glamour of a major television network.

Whatever NHP lacks in glamour, it makes up for in power. As the nation's largest owner and developer of rental housing, NHP holds enviable records. It is: (1) one of the largest owner/managers of senior citizen rental housing in the country; (2) second-largest apartment owner in the country; (3) largest developer and manager of government-assisted housing in the country; (4) fourth-largest developer of apartment property in the country; and (5) seventh-largest home builder in the country.

Why is this important? Because Buffet built his legendary reputation and $2-billion dollar net worth buying value-oriented, long-term investments. His $36-million interest in NHP is another optimistic note for the future of real estate.

Of course, when professionals like Holloway and Buffet buy investment-grade real estate, they don't expect to double their money overnight. They understand the concept of property appreciation, and they know it takes time to manage and develop property to its optimum market value.

Every dollar added to the bottom line increases the market value of the property $16 or $17. Those increases translate into substantial gains on large properties. If you add $500,000 to the bottom line of an office building, you increase its market value $8 million to $8.5 million.

The ability to "create value" makes real estate attractive to knowledgeable investors at all levels. The added value translates into substantial capital appreciation and delivers profits that are hard to match in any other type of investment.

HISTORICAL HOME RUNS

How does real estate's profit potential translate into dollars and cents for investors? The following are good examples of how quality real estate performs.

The Japanese Yen for Real Estate

The Japanese continue to make headlines as they snap up prime U.S. properties. In 1987, they purchased the Washington headquarters of *U.S. News & World Report* from real estate developer/publisher Mortimer B. Zuckerman. They paid $80 million for a 5-year-old building assessed at $30,190,200.

To sweeten the deal, *U.S. News* signed a 20-year lease on the property and the Japanese gave Mr. Zuckerman an option to repurchase the property in 20 years.

Pan Am's Property Takes Off

In 1980, Pan Am sold its prestigious Park Avenue headquarters for $400 million. The $270-million profit—a gain of more than 200 percent—was more than the airline earned the previous 10 years flying planes.

Lee Iacocca's Big Blunder

In 1979, Lee Iacocca sold all Chrysler's downtown dealership real estate for $90-million to help the ailing automaker pay its bills. Later, just to keep dealerships in strategic locations, Chrysler bought *half* the real estate back for $180 million—twice the price!

In all fairness to Iacocca, he was hired to save Chrysler—not make money in real estate. Chrysler desperately needed cash and Iacocca's strategy turned the automaker into a classic American success story. It makes an interesting footnote that he raised much-needed capital by converting hard assets—real estate—into cash quickly.

The Reichmanns Take Manhattan

In 1977, Canada's Reichmann family purchased eight Manhattan office buildings for $320 million. It was a bold move. New York City was on the brink of bankruptcy. Real estate was on the rocks. Many industry experts said the deal would be the Reichmann's Waterloo. By 1987, the value of the buildings topped $2.5-billion.

SMALL INVESTORS SCORE BIG, TOO

How can this type of profit potential produce big winners for small investors? Through quality real estate investments on Wall Street—where small investors can participate in big deals the same way they invest in big corporations.

Many small investors have already enjoyed healthy real estate profits on Wall Street. More are staking their claim everyday. We shall now take a closer look at how several investors with sound game plans picked profitable stocks for their real estate portfolios.

John sells houses for a national real estate firm. He knew the high interest rates of the early 1980s created a pent-up demand for houses. He felt sure home-building stocks would soar once rates fell and people began buying houses again. John did some quick research on major home-building companies. When rates began falling, he made his move.

In January 1985, he invested $5000 in Hovnanian, a New Jersey home-building firm with an outstanding record of sales and profit. By December, the stock had risen 187 percent. John cashed in his chips, pocketing a $9,350 profit in just 12 months.

If you think that's an exceptional gain, you're right. It certainly doesn't happen every day or every year. But even if John had chosen another home-building company he could still have made a handsome profit.

During the same time period other builders enjoyed record gains, too. For example, Ryan Homes rose 71.76 percent, Lennar climbed 65.35 percent, Ryland Group jumped 54.24 percent, General Homes scored 44.68 percent, and Centex Corp recorded a 39.41 percent gain.

You don't have to be in the real estate industry, like John, to identify important trends. Carole, an internist with a group health association, knew America had a growing need for quality nursing homes. She was too busy caring for patients to buy or manage real estate on her own, but she wanted an investment play in the health field.

Carole's broker recommended several nursing home stocks and sent her some financial data to review on each company. Early in 1985 Carole put her $2000 IRA contribution into Beverly Investment Properties, a Los Angeles-based equity real estate investment trust specializing in the ownership of health-care facilities.

In just 12 months the stock rose 26.97 percent. Carole's original $2000 investment had grown to $2539.40 in her fully tax-sheltered retirement account. Carole is holding her stock as a long-term investment since she's very bullish on the nation's need for nursing homes.

Dan took a different route to riches in the stock market. A CPA with a large regional accounting firm that represents several major real estate developers, Dan has seen their tax returns and knows the investment potential of quality real estate. He wants to profit from opportunities in commercial development.

Since he is pretty savvy with numbers, Dan spent several evenings in the local library checking stock reports in the *Value Line Investment Survey*. He decided on Southmark Corporation, a Texas developer with a strong track record. Within a year his stock rose 75 percent.

But Southmark wasn't the only profit play in commercial development. Cousins Properties rose 46.25 percent and Koger Properties gained 25.96 percent. During the same period of time, real estate financial services prospered too. Greentree Acceptance scored a 60.14 percent gain while Pan American Mortgage rose an impressive 71.07 percent.

Real estate investment trusts (REITs) offered attractive rewards as well. The Washington Real Estate Investment Trust increased 36.24 percent, Bradley REIT gained 44.95 percent, and HMG Property Investors rose 49.29 percent. Two racetrack REITs, Hollywood Park and Santa Anita Realty, clocked in with 36.42 percent and 40.43 percent wins, respectively. Obviously, your chance of winning at the races is better on Wall Street than at the $2 window at the track.

Will real estate continue to be a winner on Wall Street? Yes! For investors who buy value, and have patience, Wall Street is a gold mine for knowledgeable prospectors.

REAL ESTATE'S PROFITABLE FUTURE

Why Real Estate Prices Will Rise

There are five reasons quality real estate will continue to be a top-notch, long-term performer. First, the supply–demand balance is now in the second of four stages of the traditional real estate growth cycle. The four stages are: (1) development, (2) overbuilding, (3) adjustment, and (4) acquisition.

At present, most markets have an ample supply of space available for lease or sale. Despite this fact, developers continue to break ground for new projects because they have been in the planning stage several years. However, construction is now slowing down. In 1987, it declined 30 percent from the previous year. By mid-1988, the real estate cycle will move into the adjustment phase as developers delay further development plans until the market absorbs the majority of the current space.

Between 1990 and 1995, the vacancy rates in most metropolitan markets will be low enough to support new projects. However, it will take three to five years to develop new space from start to finish. That is because developers need two to three years to acquire a suitable site, obtain the required zoning, and present architectural plans for approval by government officials and citizens groups, followed by another 18 to 24 months to actually build the project.

In the meantime, the existing space is absorbed and demand begins to outstrip supply. As with any commodity, when there are more buyers than sellers, the price rises. In real estate, that means rent increases, which ultimately boost the bottom line and the market value of the property.

The second reason centers around the institutionalization of the real estate market. Not too many years ago, real estate was viewed as inappropriate for institutional portfolios—too risky since it was an entrepreneurial business, localized and tax shelter oriented. Institutions limited their participation to long-term mortgages on investment-grade buildings with AAA tenants. They were content to take a steady, fixed-rate return and leave the risks of ownership and development to developers. But by the late 1970s, real estate became the fastest growing single investment asset in the institutional world.

With the rising inflation of the 1970s and the historical success of good real estate as an inflation hedge, the large insurance companies began to pour billions of dollars into quality real estate. Many now invest on a joint-venture basis with large regional developers; others have their own development teams.

Third, the arrival of institutional investors in the real estate market fueled the "securitization" of real estate. Small investors wanted a viable and affordable way to take a stake in major real estate deals. This opened the door for institutional investors to sell small pieces of their pie to individual investors.

Fourth, tax reform accelerated the trend toward securitization by forcing investors to focus on income. Thus, income-oriented real estate securities became an attractive vehicle for investors to earn current income from a stock with capital appreciation potential.

Fifth, global buyers are paying record prices for U.S. real estate. Once the preserve of local developers, syndicators, insurance companies, and pension funds, American real estate is attracting big global buyers with deep pockets. They are paying record prices for office buildings, shopping centers, hotels, and apartment complexes. These higher prices are the result of two factors: the declining dollar, which permits foreigners to spend more in dollars; and the unique investment perspectives shared by foreign buyers.

To many seasoned developers in the United States, investors from western Europe, the Middle East and Japan are naive and overpay for what they perceive as value. Actually, typical West German or Japanese investors are not focused on a 7 to 10-year investment cycle. More often, they're looking 20 to 25 years down the road. As one London investor put it, "We look at real estate as an investment for a generation." On this basis, they head for recognized value and are willing to pay top dollar for it. "Selectivity" is the key!

Inflation Is Pushing Prices Up Again

Forget government reports that indicate inflation is dead or taking a long nap. Inflation is alive and reducing your buying power every day. Government reports treat inflation as one number. In reality, inflation must be examined on a sector basis to assess its full impact on your pocketbook.

Housing is a good example. In 1987, the median price of a new house in the United States rose 21 percent—to a record $110,600. The increase wasn't limited to large cities; small towns were hit hard, too, as Table 1–1 shows.

Industry experts warn the upward price spiral has just begun. According to a study released by the National Association of Realtors, the price of the average American home will triple by the year 2000.

Real Estate Is an Essential Commodity

Most people take real estate for granted. The roof over their head is a home—not a "detached single-family dwelling" or a "condominium unit."

When they buy food, they go to the grocery store—not to a "150,000-gross-square-foot, one-story building of block and reinforced concrete." They work at their company's headquarters—not a "mid-rise office building in an industrial park zoned for office and commercial use."

Real estate is everywhere, like the sun or the air. It is an integral part of every aspect of our lives: housing, offices, shopping, workplaces, health care, even cemeteries. You cannot live without it. Since real estate is essential to our existence, there always will be a demand for quality property wherever people live or

Table 1-1
Median Sales Price of Existing Single-Family Homes

Area*	1984	1987	Increase
		(second quarter)	
Albany/Schenectady/ Troy	$52,900	$86,500	$33,600 (+64%)
Anaheim/Santa Ana** (Orange County)	$133,700	$167,300	$33,600 (+25%)
Boston	$100,000	$175,800	$75,800 (+76%)
Buffalo/Niagara Falls	$44,800	$57,000	$12,200 (+27%)
Detroit	$48,500	$66,600	$18,100 (+37%)
Hartford	$87,400	$157,000	$69,600 (+80%)
Jacksonville	$55,700	$65,800	$10,100 (+18%)
Memphis	$64,100	$76,900	$12,800 (+20%)
New York/Northern New Jersey/Long Island	$105,300	$183,000	$77,700 (+74%)
Philadelphia	$65,200	$84,400	$19,200 (+29%)
Providence	$59,600	$109,800	$50,200 (+84%)
Rochester	$59,700	$72,300	$12,600 (+21%)
San Diego**	$100,200	$127,100	$26,900 (+27%)
Washington, D.C.	$93,000	$120,400	$27,400 (+29%)
West Palm Beach/ Boca Raton/Delray Beach	$84,800	$104,300	$19,500 (+23%)

Source: National Association of Realtors

*All areas are metropolitan statistical areas (MSAs) as defined by the U.S. Office of Management and Budget. They include the named central city and surrounding suburban areas.

**Provided by the California Association of Realtors

work. More importantly, the demand for property constantly changes as people alter their lifestyles and businesses.

The elements of demand and constant change present challenges to developers: New buildings must include state-of-the-art technology in all areas. In housing, as well, these technologies allow us to live and work in a more efficient environment. All of this underscores the importance of real estate in our daily lives—one more reason this vibrant industry has a bright future.

How You Can Profit From Real Estate On Wall Street

By developing a portfolio of quality real estate stocks, you can position yourself for attractive yields in the short term and strong capital appreciation over the next three to five years.

You can choose from many different types of real estate investments on Wall Street. In this book, we'll detail them for you and show you how to pick the winners. In effect, we'll give you a menu. You pick the type of real estate and the amount of money to invest based upon your own investment appetite and goals. First, we'll explore the benefits of buying real estate on Wall Street.

2

The Benefits of Buying Real Estate on Wall Street

Wall Street is rapidly replacing Main Street as the most profitable and practical place to invest in real estate. Tax reform changed the name of the real estate game from "shelter" to "income." As investors revised their investment strategies, it didn't take them long to realize that Wall Street real estate investments are income-driven vehicles. They pay quarterly dividends and offer capital appreciation potential.

But the benefits of buying real estate on Wall Street go far beyond income and appreciation. Investors get many advantages not available to individual real estate owners. Let's take a closer look at them.

SMALL INVESTORS WELCOME

Anyone with a small nest egg can buy real estate on Wall Street. You can start building your portfolio with as little as $500 to $1000.

Buying real estate on Main Street takes a lot more cash. Twenty years ago almost anyone could buy a good rental house with as little as $500 to $1000 down. Houses in nice neighborhoods sold for $25,000 to $30,000.

Today it's a different story. If you buy an ordinary three-bedroom house in a middle-class neighborhood, chances are you'll pay at least $85,000 or more. Add another 5 percent for closing costs. If you're an investor, give the banker at least 20 percent down. That's $21,250 in cash just to get started. Even then you'll be lucky to break even at the end of the year.

What about those great "no money down" deals you've read so much about? If you've seen the newspapers lately, you know most of the no-money-down promoters are in bankruptcy—their "paper" empires are in shreds.

Albert J. Lowry is a good case in point. During the heyday of the no-money-down race to real estate riches, nobody sold the dream of wealth better than Al Lowry. His was the classic rags-to-riches story.

After leaving his native Canada, the former supermarket butcher arrived in the United States with only a few dollars in his pocket. He moved to San Francisco and began buying houses in nearby Oakland for no money down. By the time he landed on the cover of *Money* magazine in 1981, he claimed an estimated net worth of $30 million.

Lowry, a master of promotion, taught his wealth-building strategies to aspiring millionaires who paid $495 each to attend his weekend seminars. If you missed the lecture, you could always buy the book. The best selling, *How You Can Become Financially Independent by Investing in Real Estate* was followed by another book with an alluring title, *How to Become Financially Successful by Owning Your Own Business*.

Soon Lowry was pitching the potential of no-money-down real estate investing on late night television. His paid documentary, *How to be Successful in America*, usually ran opposite the Johnny Carson or David Letterman shows. Suddenly, insomniacs had a third choice: Get rich quick!

Just when it looked like Al Lowry would be the next champion on the all-time list of Successful Real Estate Investors, the pitfalls of buying rental houses with "no money down" caught up with him. Banks and other creditors demanded their money. Lowry's road to riches was paved with red ink. The man whose empire grossed $40 million between 1969 and 1985 filed for bankruptcy in 1987.

No-money-down was never a very viable concept for making steady profits in rental property. Usually, the mortgage payments, taxes, and insurance exceed the rental income.

During periods of high inflation, when houses command ever-rising prices, many investors support a negative cash flow each month in anticipation of a large gain on sale. But when inflation cools down, rental houses have to rely on rents to make them profitable. That is when investors holding a portfolio of highly leveraged real estate often see their houses of cards collapse.

Wall Street offers you another plus: Since real estate stocks can be purchased in easily affordable denominations, you can add to your portfolio whenever you have extra cash to invest. For example, instead of spending your next raise or bonus on a ski trip, send it to Wall Street. It will keep on working for you long after the winter snow melts.

LIQUIDITY

You can buy and sell real estate on Wall Street in minutes—not months. That is a big advantage if you want to lock in your profit or put your appreciation to work in a new investment opportunity.

Tapping your equity and appreciation in rental property takes patience. Even in a good market, you must wait four to six months for your money.

First, you must advertise and show your property, find a qualified buyer, negotiate a contract of sale, and wait for the buyer to get a loan. If the buyer's loan application is rejected, you must start the process all over again.

During periods of exceptionally high interest rates, like the early 1980s, real estate sellers had to carry mortgages at below-market interest rates or offer steep price discounts to get an all-cash sale. Some sellers had to sit on the sidelines several years until rates came down. On Wall Street, *you* time your transactions.

LEVERAGE: BUYING ON MARGIN

You can borrow money to buy most real estate stocks. Borrowing to buy stocks is known as leveraging your assets or "buying on margin."

Buying on margin lets you magnify your potential profit—just as mortgages do when you buy property. Here is how it works:

Assume you buy $5000 worth of stock. You put down 50 percent cash or $2500. Your brokerage firm loans you the $2500 balance at the prevailing margin account rate (which is usually somewhat lower than the rate charged by commercial banks).

Suppose the stock rises in value to $7500. You sell and take a $2500 profit. That's a 100 percent return on your $2500 investment (before deducting brokerage fees and interest charges). If you had paid all cash for your purchase, your return would be only 50 percent.

Before you buy on margin, remember this: Leverage carries higher risk. If the price of your stock drops, you'll get a "margin call" requiring you to ante up the difference in cash.

DIVERSIFICATION

Buying real estate on Wall Street offers you an opportunity to build a diversified real estate portfolio. Depending upon your financial goals, you can choose from companies with investment strategies ranging from conservative to aggressive.

You can also spread your investment dollars among different types of real estate. For example, you might buy stock in a real estate investment trust specializing in shopping centers, invest in a limited partnership that owns an office building, and put the remainder of your funds in a solid home building firm. You can create a portfolio mix tailored to your exact requirements.

You can structure your real estate stock selections to create an inflation hedge in your personal and retirement portfolios. In addition to current income and appreciation, your real estate stocks will be poised to protect your portfolio from the ravages of inflationary cycles.

PROFESSIONAL PORTFOLIO MANAGEMENT

You get three benefits from professional management:

Professional property selection. Your properties are bought and sold by real estate executives experienced in selecting, financing, and negotiating real estate transactions. They have the professional ability to evaluate market feasibility studies, prepare complex financial analyses, negotiate contracts, and obtain favorable financing at competitive rates.

Professional property management. Real estate professionals know how to manage property for maximum income and appreciation. The responsibility for day-to-day operations falls on their shoulders, not yours. If the boiler goes on the blink in your office building, you don't have to worry about finding a contractor or the money to repair it. Professional management gives you peace of mind and the time to pursue your own priorities.

Professional accounting records. When you own real estate stocks or partnerships, you get quarterly financial reports on your company and regular reports from your stock broker. You can monitor the financial progress of your investment at a glance.

When you own property individually, you often end up with a shoe box stuffed with receipts. You tally the numbers once a year—at tax time—and hope to do better next year. With professional management, you get a team of trained experts managing your money everyday, so you can sleep better every night.

OWN MAJOR LEAGUE PROPERTIES

Real estate stocks and partnerships give you an opportunity to participate in the financial benefits of owning major commercial and residential properties. Historically, only wealthy individual investors, insurance companies, and pension funds could afford to buy this type of investment-grade real estate.

What type of property can small investors own? The Empire State Building is a good example. While it is commonly said, "Harry Helmsley owns the Empire State Building," it should be added he has 3300 limited partners in the deal. Each invested $10,000 when the project was syndicated in 1961.

If office buildings aren't your cup of tea, try Boston's Faneuil Hall Marketplace or Baltimore's Inner Harbor Development. Both projects were historic renovations undertaken by the Rouse Company—a publicly traded stock with a long history of steady dividends and capital appreciation.

Do you want still more excitement? Florida's fabled Hollywood race course and California's elegant Santa Anita race track are both owned by publicly traded real estate investment trusts. In addition to the tracks, both REITs own and develop prime property nearby.

PICK THE TYPE OF PROPERTY YOU WANT

When you buy real estate on Wall Street, you can target your investment to a particular type of property. You do this by choosing a stock or a partnership that specializes in the type of property you want to own.

Here is just a sample of the type of property you can invest in on Wall Street:

Office buildings

Shopping centers

Apartment complexes

Industrial/warehouses

Land development companies

Hotels

Nursing homes/hospitals

Race tracks

Mortgage loans

Retirement housing

In addition, you can invest in real estate-related companies. These include hotel operating companies, building materials firms, construction companies, build-it-yourself retail outlets, and others. We shall outline these opportunities in detail for you in Chapter 4, "Real Estate-Related Industries."

YOU'RE IN CONTROL

You don't need anyone's approval to buy or sell real estate on Wall Street. You don't have to negotiate with surly sellers. You don't have to sit on pins and needles while bankers intimidate you with requests for endless documentation before approving your mortgage application.

On Wall Street, you decide when to buy and sell. One quick call moves you into—or out of—any stock position in minutes. You make the decisions. You call the shots. You're the boss.

3

REITs: Low Cost, High Yield Real Estate

Tax reform turned the spotlight on real estate investment trusts. These high-yielding real estate stocks are basking in the limelight as small investors snap them up for income and growth. Their popularity is easy to explain.

Commonly called REITs, these trusts are sold as publicly traded stocks and give investors just what tax reform ordered—an income-oriented investment. Equally important, they are highly liquid, offer strong appreciation potential, and are available in affordable denominations.

Real estate investment trusts are one of the easiest and safest ways for small investors to own quality income-producing real estate. Let's take a closer look at REITs and how you can benefit from owning them.

WHAT IS A REIT?

REITs are similar to mutual funds. (However, unlike mutual funds, REITs own long-term investments.) To get the full benefit of long-term appreciation, REITs are best held several years at least. They own a portfolio of income-producing property or mortgages, sometimes both. The primary goal is high current income and capital appreciation, making them a popular "total return" investment.

TAX REFORM BENEFITS REITs

Although many real estate investments were affected by tax reform, and investment strategies were altered to reflect the new emphasis on income, REITs grew more popular without making any changes. Reform gave them "tax appeal."

The new tax law reduced two major real estate investment benefits: depreciation and excess writeoffs against salary and other income. REITs came up winners on both items, for two reasons.

First, depreciation was extended from 19 years to 27.5 years for residential property and 31.5 years for commercial property. This change left REITs unscathed since they have always followed a federally mandated 35-year depreciation schedule.

Second, writeoffs from passive investments cannot exceed income from passive investments. Again, REITs remained unaffected since they do not pass any tax losses through to shareholders. REITs are portfolio income. The limit on passive loss deductions, combined with lower tax rates, actually increased the demand and value of these income-oriented investments.

In the final analysis, tax reform is a plus for REITs. The following section takes a closer look at the benefits of owning REITs and explains how they can be a plus for your portfolio.

INVESTMENT ADVANTAGES

No Corporate Taxes

Unlike most stocks, REITs avoid double taxation. They pay no corporate income tax. Income is taxed only once, at the investor level, which is especially appealing at today's lower individual and higher corporate tax rates.

To qualify as a REIT, and enjoy this tax benefit, the law requires the REIT to:

1. pay at least 95 percent of its taxable income in dividends;
2. generate at least 75 percent of its income from real estate or mortgages it owns;
3. buy real estate or mortgages for long-term investment.

REITs Generate High Current Income

Real estate investment trusts are income-driven vehicles. They pay regular cash dividends, just like any other stock. However, since they pay no corporate income tax they have more money with which to pay dividends. This gives investors a higher total return on their investments, because earnings are taxed only once—-at the investor level.

Highly Liquid Investments

Real estate investment trusts are the most liquid real estate investment you can buy. They issue shares of stock, which are traded on all the major stock exchanges. You can buy or sell REIT stocks any day of the week.

Affordably Priced Investments

Shares can be purchased in affordable denominations. Many attractive REIT stocks trade in the $10 to $30 price-per-share range.

That means you can start building your real estate portfolio with as little as $500 to $1000. When you have additional money to invest, you can easily increase your current position in a favorite REIT or diversify into another type of REIT.

Dividend Reinvestment Programs Available

Dividend reinvestment programs (DRPs) give investors an opportunity to compound their earnings by automatically converting quarterly cash dividends into additional shares of stock. Instead of coming to you in a check every quarter, your dividend is used to buy more stock in the company. This has several advantages. For example:

1. Your earnings compound. Every dollar reinvested brings you more dividends and increases your base for capital appreciation potential.

2. You keep your money invested in a high-yielding growth stock, which is important because it is not easy to invest odd sums of money, like a $50 dividend check, in an attractive investment.

3. You can buy additional shares of stock at little or no cost. Dividend reinvestment programs reduce or eliminate the commission you usually pay when you buy and sell stock. This dollar savings keeps more of your money working and, ultimately, boosts the total return on your investment.

4. You can buy fractional shares of stock. For example, if your quarterly cash dividend is $54 and the current stock price per share is $12, you can buy 4-1/2 additional shares of stock—something you couldn't do on any of the stock exchanges.

5. Some dividend reinvestment programs let you buy stock at a discount to the current market value. A few REITs, but not all, offer this additional benefit.

6. Dividend reinvestment programs encourage savings. Many investors deposit their dividends in their checking accounts with good intentions of reinvesting the money, but it rarely happens. Dividends arrive just when investors seem to need a little extra cash. The December check helps pay holiday bills, the March check comes in handy at tax time, the June check goes on vacation, and so on.

When you reinvest your dividends, you pay yourself first. Some DRPs permit shareholders to invest extra cash with any quarterly dividend reinvestment.

Appreciation Potential

Like all good real estate investments, REITs offer appreciation potential. When real estate is managed for maximum appreciation, the investor profits two ways.

First, the yield on the investment increases when rents rise and cash flow increases. This happens when demand for space permits management to raise rents or when management improves a property.

Second, your capital appreciates too. Since income-producing properties are sold on yield, every dollar management adds to the bottom line of a property's operating statement increases the price at which the property could be sold or refinanced.

For example, if an office building produces $1 million in cash flow after operating expenses, a buyer looking for a 10 percent return would expect to pay $10 million cash for that building.

If prudent management increased the cash flow by $150,000 to $1,150,000 the same buyer would pay $11,150,000 for the same building. That additional $150,000 in income added $1,150,000 to the value of the property.

An Inflation Hedge

When inflationary cycles occur, well located real estate comes up a big winner. Rising rents and investor demand for hard assets boost property prices.

Investors benefit two ways. First, rising rents increase operating profits, which REITs pass along to shareholders in the form of bigger dividends. Second, inflation increases the market (sales) value of the REIT's assets. Since income producing properties are bought and sold on yield, every dollar added to the "bottom line" boosts the book value of the stock.

Tax Shelter Potential

When you buy property on your own or through a limited partnership, you enjoy limited tax deductions. Although REITs do not pass any writeoffs through to shareholders, they do offer two potential tax advantages.

1. **Return of capital.** When a REIT sells a property that has appreciated in value, a portion of the sale price is usually designated as a "return of capital" and is not subject to tax.

    For purposes of illustration, let's assume a REIT buys a shopping center for $5 million. The REIT opts to assume an existing $2.5-million mortgage and pays the balance in cash.

    In five years, the REIT sells the shopping center for $7 million—a profit of $2 million. After paying off the original $2.5-million mortgage, the REIT opts to distribute the remaining $4.5 million in sales proceeds to shareholders.

    For tax purposes, only the $2-million capital gain is taxable. The other $2.5 million is a "return of capital," representing the REIT's original downpayment.

    What does this mean to shareholders? Suppose the REIT has 1 million shares of stock outstanding. The $4.5-million cash distribution will equal $4.50 for each share of stock. Of the $4.50 distribution only $2.00 is taxable income. The other $2.50 is considered return of capital.

    If you owned 200 shares of stock in the REIT, you would get $900 cash. You would only pay tax on $400 (200 shares X $2.00). The other $500 (200 shares X $2.50) is a tax-free return of capital that you put in your pocket.

2. **Portfolio income.** Tax reform classified REIT income as "portfolio" (not passive) income. The new law permits investors to deduct up to $3000 per year in portfolio losses against ordinary (salary) income.

    Unlike many forms of real estate ownership, REITs do not pass any real or paper losses through to shareholders. However, portfolio losses can shelter portfolio income. Suppose you had a $2000 loss on the sale of your Careless

Chemical Company stock and a $3500 gain on the sale of your Profitable Properties REIT. You could use your $2000 loss to reduce your $3500 taxable gain, paying tax only on $1500 of your gain.

Avoid the Risks of Sole Ownership

When you buy a small rental property on your own, you are usually personally liable for the mortgage and real estate taxes. You can also be personally liable for injuries or accidents occurring on your property.

In addition, individual investors typically manage their own property, which means you are on call seven days and nights a week. When something goes wrong, you must fix it or find an expert who can. Either way, it's a major aggravation and a time-consuming chore. When you own shares in a REIT, your financial exposure is limited to the amount of money invested, and your time is your own—time you can use to relax or pick more winners on Wall Street.

HOW TO PICK THE RIGHT REIT

To pick a profitable REIT for your portfolio, remember this rule: "All REITs are not created equal." Many factors influence the quality and profit potential of a REIT: property locations, debt structure, management's ability to improve the income and value of the REIT's portfolio, local economic conditions, business trends, and, of course, the REIT's track record for delivering steady dividends and growth.

In addition, there are three different types of REITs: (1) equity, (2) mortgage, and (3) hybrid. Each type offers a different profit and risk potential, ranging from conservative to speculative. Before you invest, you must select a REIT you can live with financially and psychologically. You want a REIT with investment goals and strategies that are in harmony with your own.

Fortunately, selecting a quality REIT is much easier than it sounds. Basically, you need to answer just three questions:

1. What are the REIT's investment goals?

2. What are the potential rewards and risks?

3. What are the hallmarks of a quality REIT?

To help you answer those questions, we've prepared a summary of equity, mortgage, and hybrid REITs that should let you pick REITs like a pro.

Equity REITs

An equity REIT owns a portfolio of income-producing properties. Some equity REITs specialize in a particular type of property, like shopping centers or apartments. Others own a diversified portfolio that includes many different types of property (office buildings, warehouses, apartments, hotels, shopping centers, etc.). Many also concentrate their investments in a specific region of the country.

In general, equity REITs avoid heavy debt. Most buy property with little or no financing. By keeping their debt at low to moderate levels, equity REITs keep their breakeven point low. This lets them make attractive investments without holding excess cash or doing a new underwriting.

Rewards and Risks

Equity REITs hold the best industry record for regular dividends, steady growth, and capital appreciation. Their focus on ownership combined with low debt allows them to manage properties to deliver attractive yields for maximum appreciation with low financial risk.

An equity REIT with low-to-moderate debt and a successful track record is the most conservative type of REIT you can buy.

The risk is relatively low, and the potential for growing dividends and capital appreciation ranges from very good to excellent.

Guidelines for Selecting a Quality Equity REIT

When you buy an equity REIT, concentrate on quality. Avoid being lured into a new offering that is looking for big profits in distressed property or a troubled REIT that hopes to cure its old problems by issuing new stock.

Real estate is a cyclical industry, and the best way to cushion yourself against any softness in the market is to own quality property. First-class real estate consistently outperforms other property in all economic climates. Quality property may not offer glamour and excitement, but it usually offers hard-to-beat returns.

Before you invest in an equity REIT, spend a little time doing some homework. Compare the REITs you are considering against the following checklist.

1. **Does the REIT have a record of steady growth and regular dividends?** If not, consider this a red flag. If the record is inconsistent, management, rather than a poor market, is probably to blame. Professionals tend to buy and manage property for fairly consistent returns under varying economic climates.

2. **Are dividends paid from operating profits?** They should be. REITs that pay dividends from the sale of new stock, refinancing proceeds, or capital gains profits may not be producing a stable income stream. A well managed REIT produces a genuine cash flow that is used to pay regular dividends.

3. **If the REIT has sold property, has it made a profit?** Unless the REIT is buying and selling property at a profit, management is not doing a professional job. Of course, management may elect to hold the property in anticipation of future growth or refinance the property if it has appreciated substantially. However, an occasional capital gain distribution is a sign of good financial health and an indication that management is effectively increasing the value of the REIT's assets.

4. **What is the debt-to-equity ratio?** In simple terms, what is the REIT's total debt as a percentage of its total assets? For example, if the REIT owns properties with a current market value of $20 million, and has a total of $15 million in debt, the debt-to-equity ratio is 3:1. The properties are 75 percent mortgaged ($15M divided by $20M = .75 or 75%).

    Avoid equity REITs with steep debt-to-equity ratios. Highly leveraged REITs face greater risk. If vacancies increase, heavy mortgage payments can send cash flow into a tailspin. A declining cash flow will be reflected in the dividend.

    Look for moderate leverage—50 percent or, preferably, less. You want your management team to focus on performance and profit—not on scraping up enough cash to make the next mortgage payment.

5. **Does the REIT make capital improvements to the properties in its portfolio?** A well managed REIT improves cash flow through a regular program of capital improvements designed to help increase rents and attract desirable tenants. The improved cash flow will produce more income for dividend distribution and create capital appreciation that should benefit investors when a property is sold or refinanced.

6. **Does the REIT have a first-class management team?** The quality and experience of management is critical to the REIT's ability to deliver steadily increasing dividends and to manage properties for capital appreciation. Top managers should own stock in the REIT so they have a vested interest in seeing the REIT perform profitably.

Mortgage REITs

These REITs hold mortgages on income producing properties owned and managed by others. They do not actually own property.

A mortgage REIT may put all its eggs in one basket, like Rockefeller Center Properties, Inc. Its sole asset is a mortgage secured by Rockefeller Center in the heart of Manhattan. Other mortgage REITs own a diversified portfolio of mortgages.

The primary goal of mortgage REITs is high current income. Because they typically incur greater risk and trade more like bonds, they are subject to greater fluctuations in market value. Mortgage REITs historically pay dividends 2 to 3 percent higher than equity REITs. The following is a closer look at those higher yields and the risks that go with them.

Rewards and Risks

A top mortgage REIT can give investors an exceptionally attractive rate of return competitive with bonds. Today many mortgage REITs hedge their bets—and maximize their total returns—by negotiating "participating mortgages." In addition to regular monthly mortgage payments, participating mortgages give the REIT upside potential because they get a percentage of the increase in cash flow or a percentage of the profit when the property is sold.

As with most investment, higher yield carries higher risk. Mortgage REITs are riskier than equity REITs because they own debt, not real property. If the property owner cannot make the mortgage payments, the REIT's income could drop dramatically, forcing the REIT to cut dividends or stop paying them altogether until the property is turned around, or sold. Of course, mortgage REITs always have the option of foreclosing on troubled property, but that won't restore the lost income. It may take several years to get the property fully leased and operating profitably. If the REIT forecloses and then sells the property, they have to offer the buyer an attractive discount to purchase a troubled property.

Guidelines for Selecting a Quality Mortgage REIT

Despite the greater risk generally associated with mortgage REITs, they can be good, high-yielding investments. The key to enjoying their higher yields while protecting your capital is to select a mortgage REIT that employs a prudent lending policy, which means the REIT structures its mortgage portfolio to minimize risk and maximize return.

Before you invest in a mortgage REIT, compare its lending policy against the following checklist. If the REIT doesn't measure up, don't buy it.

1. **Select a REIT with strong sponsorship.** Be certain the REIT is advised by a financial institution with REIT lending experience. Be certain the REIT's managers have experience and a successful track record in managing a mortgage REIT portfolio. The sponsor's experience is outlined in the prospectus and the annual reports.

2. **Look for moderate leverage.** The REIT should make first mortgages that do not exceed 60 percent of the property's value. When a mortgage REIT finances more than 75 percent of a property's value, it moves into the high-risk zone.

3. **Avoid REITs that own second mortgages.** The properties involved are nearly always overfinanced, which means the owner is usually straining to make mortgage payments. To make matters worse, the second mortgage is subordinate to the first mortgage. The REIT's entire investment could be wiped out if the owner of the first mortgage forecloses on the property. Second mortgages are a red flag. Avoid them like the plague.

4. **Reduce your risk with "participating mortgages."** Buying a mortgage REIT that owns participating mortgages reduces your risk two ways. First, since the REIT has a "piece of the action," trust managers will structure a mortgage that is likely to produce an attractive profit for it. Second, the participation feature can enhance your total return, allowing you to benefit from inflation, property appreciation, or other favorable market developments.

5, **Don't buy REITs that finance new construction.** These are super high risk investments. If the building doesn't lease up on schedule, it could be months or years before the developer can make the mortgage payments. In the meantime, the mortgage REIT suffers, having given the developer millions of dollars without yet getting any interest on its investment. Even worse, its capital is in jeopardy. The REIT could have part or all of its investment at risk.

6. **Buy only REITs that make mortgages on existing properties with a proven track record.** Those buildings generate an established cash flow sufficient to meet the mortgage pay-

ments and pay the owners a respectable return. When financed with a 60 to 70 percent mortgage, they can be very sound investments for both the mortgage REIT and the property owners.

Hybrid REITs

Hybrid REITs are a combination of the equity and the mortgage REIT. They own a diversified portfolio of income-producing properties and mortgages.

The mixture of property and mortgages gives the hybrid an opportunity to deliver a higher yield than the equity REIT with more upside potential and lower risk than the mortgage REIT. The property provides a conservative anchor and a good capital appreciation play for the REIT. The mortgages give the REIT high current income to help boost the current yield and total return for the investor.

Rewards and Risks

A well managed hybrid REIT gives investors the best of both worlds: ownership of quality real estate and higher yields from mortgages. Since the REIT owns both properties and mortgages, the level of risk varies with the portfolio mix.

Assuming the REIT owns good properties and mortgages, the level of risk rises in proportion to the percent of mortgages in the REIT''s portfolio. For example, a REIT with 80 percent property and 20 percent mortgages would be lower risk than a REIT with 60 percent property and 40 percent mortgages.

Guidelines for Selecting a Quality Hybrid REIT

Since a hybrid REIT is only as good as the properties and mortgages in its portfolio, you should take a careful look at both elements before investing. You can do that easily by reviewing the following points in the annual report:

1. **What is the ratio of property to mortgages?** A low risk portfolio would contain about 70 percent property and 30

percent mortgages. If mortgages equal 50 percent of the portfolio, you are looking at a medium risk. Once the mortgages top 70 percent, or more, of the portfolio, you are in a high-risk area.

2. **Do the properties meet the guidelines for equity REITs?** Review "Guidelines for Selecting a Quality Equity REIT" earlier in this chapter.

3. **Do the mortgages measure up to the guides for mortgage REITs?** Review "Guidelines for Selecting a Quality Mortgage REIT" earlier in this chapter.

BE WARY OF NEW REITs

Since tax reform increased the appeal of REITs, new issues are coming to market every month. In general, buying into a new REIT carries a relatively higher risk.

If the REIT hasn't purchased any property yet, you will be buying into a "blind pool." There is no guarantee the REIT will be able to acquire quality property or mortgages on acceptable terms. The REIT's ability to deliver steady dividends and appreciation is unknown, and management's performance, a crucial element in the success of any REIT, is untested.

In addition, many new REITs trade below their initial offering price when they reach the open market. You may get a better price, and reduce your risk, by buying a new REIT after the stock has had several quarters in which to "settle down."

If the stock price rises, and you eventually pay a little more for a quality investment, think of the difference as an insurance premium. You reduced your risk by delaying your investment until the stock could prove its staying power in the open market.

Before investing in any new REIT, check the trust's investment objectives against the guidelines for picking a quality equity or mortgage REIT. Equally important, check the experience and track record of the trust's managers. You want a management team that knows how to buy and manage real estate profitably.

HOW WALL STREET VALUES REITs

Historically, equity REITs trade at a discount to their net asset value, because they have an indefinite life span. There is no deadline for selling the trust's assets and distributing the proceeds to the shareholders.

If you owned stock in a REIT with property currently valued at $20 million, with 1 million shares of stock outstanding, you would expect each share to be worth $20. Rarely so. A high-quality REIT might trade at $18 a share—a 10 percent discount to the market value. A lower quality REIT would trade at a larger discount.

In general, the market value of an equity REIT is determined by a combination of the current yield and Wall Street's assessment of the REIT's growth potential. Obviously, a REIT with a steady dividend and strong growth prospects will trade at a higher price than a REIT with an uneven performance and doubtful growth potential.

Mortgage REITs are valued somewhat differently. Since they own high-yielding debt and offer only modest (if any) upside potential, they trade like bonds. Consequently, their prices are subject to the same market fluctuations as bonds. When interest rates go up, their prices go down. Likewise, when interest rates go down, their prices go up.

Hybrid REITs are valued on the profit potential of both investments in their portfolio: equities and mortgages. Obviously, if a hybrid REIT owns 80 percent equities, it will trade more in line with equity REITs, but at a slight premium for the mortgages in its portfolio. If the hybrid REIT is top-heavy with mortgages, its yield will more closely approximate the value of a mortgage REIT.

SOME REITs ARE SELF-LIQUIDATING

A new breed of REIT in the stock market today is called a FREIT, which stands for "finite real estate investment trust." A FREIT differs from a traditional REIT in one respect. It has a specific life span, ranging anywhere from seven to 10 years, at which time the portfolio is liquidated and the proceeds distributed to the current shareholders.

Advocates of FREITs claim they are better than REITs, because the sale of the real estate gives investors the full appreciated value of their investment. They claim traditional REITs often own appreciated real estate carried on their books at historically low costs, making it hard for shareholders to recognize the true value of their investment unless all properties are sold.

Opponents voice an equally compelling argument. Namely, real estate is a cyclical industry. To maximize the investor's return, property should be sold in a strong market—in a seller's market—rather than according to an arbitrarily set schedule.

By selecting a liquidation date seven to 10 years away, a FREIT runs the risk of getting caught in a weak market—a buyer's market. If that happens, the FREIT will probably get far less for its property than it might if it had the option of waiting to sell in a stronger market.

Obviously, if you buy a FREIT that sells at the top of the market, you're in clover. But if you get caught in a market downturn, you'll be lucky to break even.

Our recommendation: Avoid FREITs. If you want a liquid investment in quality real estate, buy stock in one or more equity REITs. Historically, well managed equity REITs have appreciated handsomely. Equity REITs will give you steady income and attractive appreciation potential with less risk than a FREIT.

COULD REITs TAKE A NOSE-DIVE?

During the 1970s about a dozen REITs made headlines when they suffered setbacks after financing highly speculative projects in overbuilt markets. Most were mortgage or construction and development (C&D) REITs. Abandoning sound investment policies, they made high-flying loans that fell flat.

However, during that same period, many solid equity REITs prospered. They owned moderately leveraged, prime properties in strong markets. They followed a prudent investment policy under the guidance of seasoned real estate executives. They weathered the weak market with their dividends intact. Most continue to set enviable records in the REIT industry.

Today the go-go investment psychology of the 70s is gone. REIT executives employ far more conservative investment policies, starting with less leverage and more equity. Many REITs now limit leverage to 25 to 50 percent, some even less.

In addition, more REITs are concentrating on equity investments and cutting back or eliminating mortgage lending. REITs that do make mortgages are reducing their risk by requiring larger downpayments and variable-interest rate or participating mortgages.

WHERE TO GET MORE INFORMATION ON REITs

You'll find a list of publicly traded REITs in Appendix A of this book. We've included the name, address, exchange and trading symbol of each REIT.

For additional information, start with the public library. Most carry *Standard & Poor's Stock Reports* and the *Value Line Investment Survey*. Both publications cover larger REITs.

For analysis of a broader range of REITs, the *Real Estate Stock Monitor* reviews over 100 national and regional REITs. It is published by the investment banking firm of Alex. Brown & Sons, Inc., 135 East Baltimore Street, Baltimore, Maryland 21202. Telephone: 301/727-1700.

Another excellent information source is Audit's *Realty Stock Review*, a twice-monthly investment newsletter covering over 150 stocks of REITs, homebuilders, investment builders, realty services, and mortgage companies.

Audit publishes a companion report, the *Realty Stock Digest*, which provides news and ideas for investors and real estate professionals. *Digest* departments include "News," "Earnings/ Dividends," "Wall Street Analysts' Reports," "Insider Reports," and "Proxy Digest."

For subscription information for the *Realty Stock Review* or the *Realty Stock Digest*, contact Audit Investments, Inc., 136 Summit Avenue, Suite 200, Montvale, New Jersey 07645. Telephone: 201/ 358-2735.

In addition, you can get general information on REITs from the National Association of Real Estate Investment Trusts (NAREIT), 1101 17th Street, N. W., Washington, D.C. 20036. Telephone: 202/785–8717.

Also, you can find much useful information in the quarterly and annual reports issued by REITs. Ask your stockbroker to get copies for you, or write directly to the REIT. You can get their addresses from our listing in Appendix A. To help you get started we have included a brief description of 16 REITs in Appendix B, "REIT Sampler."

4

Real Estate-Related Industries

The real estate industry that is exclusive of REITs, mutual funds, and partnerships is probably the most diverse group in American business. There are four general types: (1) the credit cyclicals (so-called because their fortunes rise or fall on the basis of interest rates) such as building material companies, mobile homes manufacturers, and home builders; (2) forest products companies that supply the lumber and plywood for building; (3) the hotel/motel group, more properly called "lodging" stocks on Wall Street; and (4) retirement housing.

CREDIT CYCLICALS

Overall, real estate construction is a cyclical industry and so categorized on Wall Street as a "credit cyclical." When the economy is hit with interest rates high, and mortgage money is in short supply, housing begins to suffer. On the other hand, toward the end of a downturn, interest rates reach more attractive levels, savings rise, the Federal Reserve Board increases the money supply, and home mortgages become more affordable. As a result, home building activity increases and signals an upturn in the economy. For example, in the fall of 1982, construction activity signaled the end of a 2-year recession. Thus, this interest-rate-sensitive group should be watched closely as an indicator of economic cycles.

Construction spending accounts for roughly 10 percent of the gross national product, making the industry one of the economy's most important sectors. Since stimulation from the Federal government may create an artificial swing in the housing start figures, investors must be aware of government stimulus programs for housing. A shift in housing trends—from suburb to city or from single-unit to multiple-dwelling housing—also must be watched. These trends will have a significant impact on the types of housing to be built and building materials in demand. Population shifts, such as the rush to the sun belt, also can make or break regional companies. Significant shifts in Federal tax policy, which would affect the deductibility of interest and taxes on real estate, or a removal of tax incentives for construction of low-income housing, would also have a significant impact on this sector.

Building Materials

Building materials manufacturers, retailers, and wholesalers comprise one of the major credit cyclicals groups. Renovation of older homes is a key segment of the building industry. It is from this sector that the industry derives a stable and continuing revenue base. Those firms that supply the remodeling market have generally better records of consistent growth as compared with home-building companies, whose stock prices have been historically volatile.

The suppliers of building materials such as lumber, plywood, cement, gypsum, glass, and paint have varied potential, depending on their market mix (new housing versus renovation), on their proximity to their markets, and the adaptability of the product to new construction methods and requirements. Those companies that specialize in retailing building supplies, particularly to the do-it-yourself market, have compiled especially impressive records of growth. Makers of products that have application in energy conservation should be in an excellent position in the future as energy prices rise. These could include the manufacturers of insulation, storm doors and windows, thermal glass, weather stripping, and thermostats.

Among the major manufacturers and suppliers of building materials would be companies involved in:

Lumber and plywood

Cement

Gypsum

Paint

Insulation

Glass

Storm doors and windows

Weather stripping, etc.

Thermostats and other controls

Retailing of building supplies, the do-it-yourself market

Names and brief descriptions of some of the representative companies in the building materials sectors are included in the following list.

Armstrong World Industries (ACK-NYSE) is a strongly financed major company, having resilient flooring as a primary product line and the largest contributor to sales and earnings. Other product lines include carpeting, furniture, and building products such as ceiling materials. The last is the most sensitive to the volatile commercial construction market. Furniture, on the other hand (Thomasville Furniture, for example), has been one of ACK's more dynamic product lines. Only a fraction (about 15 percent) of ACK's operating profits come from operations outside the United States. Company management has been alert in recent years to the maturing cycle of a number of its product areas and, consequently, has completed several acquisitions in order to complement or extend its product line.

Conservatively financed with a historically high (by industry standards) cash flow, ACK is an investment grade stock candidate to "play" the construction cycle; i.e., when rates are down and the economic outlook is for a slow-to-down economy, investors will usually find this stock on the bargain counter.

American Standard, Inc. (AST-NYSE) is a well diversified company with a long, successful operating history. In terms of investment characteristics, it would be classified as cyclical, again meaning one has to buy it on a contrary basis when rates and the economy are falling and remember to sell when economic indicators and construction starts are peaking.

The company's current product line is the result of significant restructuring accomplished in the mid 1980s, when it sold several operations and used the proceeds to repurchase stock, considerably shrinking the capitalization. Old product lines were reduced or eliminated, and new money was channeled into more promising growth areas in the high-end and renovation sectors of the air conditioning (TRANE) and plumbing market. Most experts estimate earnings growth rate for the company at about 8 to 10 percent annually. Unlike Armstrong World Products, about 60 percent of AST's profits in the building products area are earned abroad.

USG Corporation is the reformed U.S. Gypsum, with more than three quarters of its profits derived from building materials or associated items. It is a major producer of gypsum wallboard— one of the essential building materials in housing. The company also is involved in wood fiber (Masonite™), ceiling grids, suspension systems, and access floor systems for nonresidential buildings. It has streamlined operations significantly by reducing expenditures and asset dispositions. For example, 25 percent of its Canadian Gypsum Company subsidiary was sold to the public. In addition, the company completed a massive common share buyback program that enhanced earnings per share.

Financially leveraged, USG does extremely well in the early stages of the construction cycle. Historically, it has been wise to sell the stock as the economy and the cycle begin to top out.

In the miscellaneous category of building materials retailers are companies such as Scotty's and Hechinger.

Scotty's, Inc. (SHB-NYSE) is located in Florida. This company is a major retailer of building supplies and materials focused on the do-it-yourself market. Sales mix includes paint, hardware, electrical fixtures, plumbing supplies, and lumber. To a lesser extent these retail outlets also service building contractors and the professional trade.

Hechinger Company (HECHB-OTC) is similar to Scotty's in operation and market focus, and operates do-it-yourself home centers up and down the eastern seaboard, but mainly in the middle Atlantic states.

The final group of building materials companies for investment consideration is comprised of those companies manufacturing and retailing home repair materials and tools.

Sikes Corporation—ceramic floor tiles for bathrooms, hallways, kitchens. Once used exclusively for bathrooms, ceramic tile is one of the fastest growing construction materials.

AFG Industries—flat glass manufacturer for windows in new homes.

Morgan Products Ltd.—distributes windows and doors.

Masco—a broad-based building products supplier manufacturing plumbing products and bathroom and kitchen fixtures as well as furniture. In a highly cyclical industry, this company has had an earnings increase each year for 30 consecutive years!

Payless Cashways, Inc.—a retail distributor of home remodeling materials and repair tools.

Stanley Works—well established manufacturer of tools and equipment for the do-it-yourself market. About a third of its business derives from the consumer sector, which offers a significant direct participation in this true growth area of the American economy.

Another credit cyclical group is the mobile home industry, sometimes referred to as "manufactured housing." Some analysts do not consider the group part of the real estate investment universe. Nevertheless, companies involved in the business do participate closely in the overall housing and interest rate cycle.

Mobile home or manufactured housing stocks should be considered as "trading" rather than investment stocks for the basic reason that the Standard & Poor's Manufactured Housing Index tends to move up and down with long term interest rates and thus these stocks are highly volatile. Companies within the group, even in the best of times, lack uniformity in terms of earnings. As a matter of fact, one of the disturbing characteristics of the group is the widely divergent earnings progress among its members. This is punctuated by the fact that in 1987, in a period of economic growth, Silvercrest, Kit Manufacturing, Nobility Homes and Cavalier Homes were showing dramatic earnings improvement, while other companies such as Connor Corp., Ockla, Vintage and De-Rose were in difficulty. Connor filed Chapter 11 bankruptcy proceedings and Ockla reported a large loss and financial irregularities for the fiscal year ending February 1987.

Due to such economic factors as shipping cost and varying state building codes, manufactured housing companies are forced to remain regional in scope. Recently, industry strength was noted in the Northeast and in Midwestern states such as Michigan, Indiana, and Ohio. The Southeast and Southwest continued to show sharply declining demand. This represents a dramatic change from the conditions in the early 1980s when sharp growth was registered in the Southeast and Southwest.

Leaders in the industry have long contended that the lack of secondary financing for mobile home loans was a major drawback. An important event for the stabilization of manufactured housing was the formation of MH Conduit Corporation to facilitate access to secondary financing markets. The Manufactured Housing Institute, with the cooperation of nine manufacturers and lenders, formed the new corporation in June 1987. Major manufacturers in the founding group include Fleetwood, Champion, Clayton, Oakwood, Palm Harbor, and Cavalier. The new corporation will package mortgage-backed securities to be sold to pension funds, insurance companies, foreign investors, and others who would not generally purchase manufactured home loans. It is expected that Conduit will provide a large and steady source of financing capital and will encourage lenders to enter the manufactured home mortgage market more freely, knowing there is access to a secondary market when they want to reduce their direct investment in manufactured home loans.

In summary, the manufactured housing business is a highly competitive one, characterized by excess capacity with accompanying shakeout and consolidation, and continuing problems with repossessions. Over the longer term, the slowdown in apartment construction reflecting the effect of the 1986 Tax Reform Act and the anticipated rent increases should produce increasing demand for manufactured homes. A list of manufactured housing stocks with some specific commentary on each is provided in Table 4–1.

Homebuilders

Another industry segment of the credit cyclical group, the homebuilders group and its member companies, can best be described as on-site builders of single-family homes. The economics are tied to demographics as well as fluctuations in mortgage interest rates. Accordingly, growth upgrading to larger homes, and demand for second homes are major factors in assessing the attraction of these stocks. Inflation, current and anticipated, is also a consideration, since it has affected not only demand but also mortgage interest rates. Accordingly, the two most important components in forecasting the future of this group are demand and affordable interest rates.

Buy these stocks to sell. When mortgage interest rates begin to edge upward, and the construction and housing cycles start to peak, you should sell your holdings in housing stocks.

Are housing stocks worth all this anxiety? You bet. From 1982 through 1986, an index of 15 building stocks appreciated fivefold!

In terms of stock prices, a review of history tells us that homebuilding stocks generally bottom out when the monthly rate of change in building permits rises 20 percent or more. That is usually a good time to consider purchasing these stocks, since they are probably priced most attractively on a price–earnings ratio. Selling should be considered when the monthly rate of change in building permits begins to fall 15 percent or more.

Table 4–1
Manufactured Housing Stocks

Name	Where Traded	Comment
Fleetwood Enterprises	FLE-NYSE	Recreational vehicle sales in a strong uptrend; manufactured housing sales were down; good record of annual dividend rate increases.
Champion Home Builders (Champion Enterprises)	CHB-ASE	In February, 1987, approved corporate reorganization establishing a holding company for company's various businesses and creating a reverse stock split.
Coachman Industries	COA-NYSE	One of the more efficient operators.
Redman Industries	RE-NYSE	Sales have been growing past several years but profits flat.
Skyline Corp.	SKY-NYSE	Company continues to be a strong cash generator and has nearly $9 per share in cash and temporary investments on the balance sheet.
Zimmer Corp.	ZIM-ASE	In addition to manufactured housing sales, the company has completed the sale of its Black Fin Yacht subsidiary for $12 million and has three manufacturing facilities for sale with a goal of eliminating debt and again becoming profitable.
Clayton Homes	CMH-NYSE	Company is experiencing strong growth in its independent dealer network.
Nobility Homes	NOBH-OTC	Revenues have been up strongly in recent years.

Table 4–1 continued

Name	Where Traded	Comment
Cavalier Homes	CAVH-OTC	In January 1987, Cavalier completed the purchase of six manufacturing facilities from Brigadier Homes, a subsidiary of U.S. Home Corporation, for $4.2 million, This acquisition made Cavalier the seventh largest manufacturer.

Some of the representative companies in this group, with brief comments on each, follow:

Kaufman & Broad (KB-NYSE) is among the largest home-builders. When things are good, K&B stock (as a most efficient producer of residential housing) can be very, very good. K&B began to develop a nationwide operation during the boom housing years of the 1960s and early 1970s. The company is focused in strong markets including California and other growth markets of the western United States plus the East Coast.

U.S. Home (UH-NYSE) is one of the major on-site builders of single-family homes. Nearly 70 percent of operations are located in the sun belt portion of the United States.

Pulte Home (PHM-NYSE) is another large builder of single-family homes, townhouses, and condominiums with concentration in the moderately priced category. Financing of new construction is most conservative—no second mortgages are accepted and the company does not speculate in raw land. ICM Mortgage, an unconsolidated mortgage banking subsidiary, provides the considerable mortgage financing.

MDC Holdings (MDC-NYSE), Denver-based, constructs, sells, and finances residential housing as well as purchases and develops land for future use. While operations historically have been concentrated in the Denver area, they have branched out to other parts of Colorado, Arizona, Florida, California, Texas, and Washington, D.C.

General Homes (GHO-NYSE) manufactures and sells moderately priced single-family homes in Houston and other regions of the south including Dallas, New Orleans, Tampa, Orlando, and Phoenix.

Killearn Properties, Inc. (KPI-ASE) constructs homes and develops planned communities primarily in the vicinity of Tallahassee, Florida and Henry County, Georgia, two areas of good steady growth.

Additional homebuilder stocks worth reviewing include *Starrett Housing Corp. (SHO-ASE)*, and *Hovnanian Enterprises (HOV-ASE)*, and *Centex (CTX-NYSE)*. Centex is a Dallas-based builder that, because of its "oil patch" orientation, has seen earnings stumble since the mid 1980s. Starrett builds residential communities, housing, and commercial and industrial buildings. Hovnanian develops housing communities primarily in New Jersey, Florida, and New York. Central to stock selection of the smaller, regional builders are the economics of their region. In the case of Hovnanian, for several years their focus in the "red hot" New Jersey residential market made that stock a star performer.

Before investing, ask yourself the following questions:

1. What are the forecasts for interest rates—long and short term?

2. What are the forecasts for inflation (measured by the Consumer Price Index)? As is well known, No. 1 and No. 2 are tied together.

3. What is the outlook for residential housing for the coming year?

4. Where are company operations concentrated? At one time, the fast-growing sun belt locations—Arizona, Florida—were prized. Today, the Northeast is the top area.

5. What homebuilding companies stand to benefit from this trend?

    • Small highly leveraged companies?

- Companies with a special market niche?
- Large well financed companies?
- Companies with a regional focus?

The second major category of the real estate industry is composed of forest products companies that manufacture or fabricate the "building blocks" of the construction industry.

FOREST PRODUCTS INDUSTRY

The forest products industry is a concentrated one, with the top 10 companies accounting for about one-third of industry production. Many are organized on a vertical basis, meaning their operations range from growing and processing of trees to manufacturing the finished product. In addition, most companies produce lumber and plywood for the building and remodeling markets. The product mix can vary widely from company to company.

Enormous expenditures are required for new plants and efficient equipment. Further, expenses for the control of air and water pollution are particularly burdensome for this industry. Growing capital needs could mean slow growth in dividends in the future, as happened in the 1970s.

Additionally, you should know that lumber and plywood shipments closely follow building industry patterns. Integration (where a company can supply end products through its own timber) is important. Further, substantial timber holdings have been a valuable inflation hedge in the past. Timber values have increased more rapidly than the rate of inflation. In contrast to most other inflation hedges, trees are self-renewing with a good deal of the care and feeding performed by nature.

Location is another important factor. A forest products company's proximity to major markets has a bearing on its prospects. Because the United States as the world's low-cost timber producer should derive long-term growth from export markets, those companies nearer seaports should be particularly favored. Similarly, owners of large tracts of southern timber should do well as a result of that region's fast growth. A number of forest products companies already have shifted operations from the Northwest to the South, where timber growth exceeds harvest levels. Georgia-Pacific Corporation is a major example of this.

Despite some problems, the forest products industry represents an important sector of the economy, one that should grow in importance as other resources become scarcer. Nevertheless, the cyclical nature of its components forces investors to search for companies that have well diversified positions within the industry, command sizable market shares within several of these areas, and finally, have strong management pursuing aggressive marketing strategies. Among the companies that seem to fit within these guidelines are the two major players in the industry: Weyerhaeuser and Georgia Pacific. Both are blue chip companies.

Georgia Pacific (GP-NYSE) is the largest forest products company in the United States, the largest plywood manufacturer and a major participant in gypsum—all key building materials.

Weyerhaeuser (WY-NYSE) is the largest lumber producer in the U.S. with a significant position in pulp, linerboard, and export logs. The latter makes Weyerhaeuser a prime beneficiary of a weaker dollar.

The third group in this category of other real estate stocks is the hotel and motel group.

HOTEL AND MOTEL GROUP

The hotel and motel business (usually more elegantly referred to as the lodging industry) is not properly a real estate-oriented business despite the fact one of the major requirements of success is good, well located real estate. Actually, most of the majors have sold or repackaged their hotel properties in the form of real estate partnerships. Nevertheless, sufficient real estate assets remain for us to consider companies in this area as potentially profitable investments.

Companies such as Marriott, Prime Motor Inns, and LaQuinta are representative of this sector. Most of the hotel and motel companies own substantial real estate holdings, although there is an increasing trend toward sale and leaseback to free up capital.

Where there are long-term leases rather than property owner-ship, the investment focus should be on operational charac-teristics rather than the quality of real estate. Among the major factors to analyze is room rates on an industry basis. Over-building usually creates future pressure on room rates and profit margins.

Typical of the companies in the industry is Prime Motor Inns, which is among the largest and most profitable lodging chains. Since going public in 1969, Prime's earnings have increased steadily (at one point, increasing 34 of 35 consecutive quarters). This high growth company is a builder and operator of motor inns. Much of the company's success is due to management's ability to build motor inns at a cost lower than its competitors'. Prime's competitive edge rests on its effectiveness in site selection, tight cost control on construction and operation, and very efficient marketing of its inns to the business traveler. Prime's acquisition of Howard Johnson gave it a recognizable franchise name, 122 motor lodges and hotels, and 375 franchised motor lodges. The company has restructured the acquisition—selling some hotels and lodges while modernizing others. Coupled with this revitali-zation, the company plans to expand the Howard Johnson fran-chise network dramatically in the next several years.

Two other companies, much larger and of continuing institu-tional investor interest, are Holiday Corporation and Marriott.

Holiday Corp. (HIA-NYSE) is Holiday Inn with a different focus and a new look. The world's largest lodging business (including its licensees), it is also a major gaming company with casinos in Las Vegas, Lake Tahoe, and Reno. Historically, nearly half of its profits have derived from the gaming operations.

Marriott Corp. (MHS-NYSE) owns, operates, and manages hotels and contract food services. It is the largest player in the U.S. lodging business. Like its other large competitors in the hotel and motel business, Marriott has interests in other sectors including contract food services and the restaurant business. The company's operations include a broad range of hotel concepts, from luxury, full service hotels and moderately priced hotels to compact economy hotels.

A new breed of investment, not quite a stock, but nevertheless,

a participation in hotel operations, is the hotel limited partnership. This new investment surfaced in the wake of the Tax Reform
Act of 1986. Wall Street perceived that, while hotel partnerships
may appear to be real estate investments, they are actually hotel
operating businesses in real estate wrappers. Most of the recent
hotel partnerships are sales by owners who will continue to
operate hotels without the cost and burden of ownership. Selling
a hotel property allows the operator to manage under contract
and achieve profits while removing the debt and depreciation
associated with ownership. Further, selling the hotel property
releases capital, allowing the company to reinvest in the construction of new properties. Typical of these hotel partnerships is
Sahara Casino Partners, which is the property segment of the
Sahara and Hacienda Hotels as well as a part of their casino
operations. Both hotels are located on the Las Vegas Strip. More
than 6 million partnership units are outstanding.

Analyzing these investments requires a functional focus. For
example, casino hotels outperform commercial, resort, or family-
oriented hotels. Over 50 percent of *Hilton Hotels (HLT-NYSE)*
profit comes from its two casino hotels. Other hotel casino owner/
operators include: *Bally Manufacturing Corp. (BLY-NYSE)*; *Caesars
World (CAW-NYSE)*; *Circus Circus (CIR-NYSE)*; *Del E. Webb (WBB-
NYSE)*; *Golden Nugget (GNG-NYSE)*; *Holiday Inns (HIA-NYSE)*; and
Resorts International (RTA-ASE).

The temptation in this new investment area is to consider hotel
partnerships as high-yield investments going in with an eventual
capital gains real estate kicker. While this may be true, caution
should be exercised in a number of areas, as detailed in the
following list:

1. Check the price(s) at which the general partner is selling the
    hotel to the partnership. It might be inflated.

2. It might pay to avoid the initial offering by the broker and
    allow the partnership units to trade for several weeks or
    months to reflect the market's pricing rather than the
    underwriter's. Waiting also avoids investment loss from the
    immediate discount from the offering price that usually oc-
    curs in these types of deals.

3. Watch out for that higher than average and sometimes "guaranteed" yield. The guarantee mechanism is made possible through the use of zero coupon bond financing. Zero coupon bond financing defers payment of principal and interest, thereby allowing more cash to be available for distribution (and thus, the high yields). However, remember that zero coupons mortgage the future. Eventually they will have to be paid. Check with your broker to determine how much zero coupon financing is being used.

4. Most hotel partnerships carry guarantees from the seller or sponsor that protect investors against unexpected events and/or seasonal variations in occupancy rates. If there is such a guarantee this could have an impact on the price paid for the property. The better the guarantee the less risk and, consequently, the higher the purchase price. Too generous a guarantee is an indication the venture is highly speculative or the partnership may have overpaid for the property.

5. The hotel operator should have performance incentives to manage the property efficiently, and by the same token the operator should be penalized if income doesn't meet projections. There should be some sort of protective clause that will implement this principle.

6. The partnership sponsor and general partner have the highest of reputations combined with experience and success in this kind of investments.

RETIREMENT HOUSING

The retirement housing industry totals $2.5 billion per year and is still growing. It is an ever present reminder of the changing demographics of the American population. While most retirement housing is developed for and by nonprofit organizations, particularly those with religious affiliations, private enterprise has an increasing share. Significant private enterprises involved in retirement housing are hotel management companies (Marriott, Hyatt, and Del E. Webb Corp.) and hospital and nursing home chains such as Manor Care and Hospital Corporation of America.

By 1990, developers and nonprofit organizations will have spent over $33 billion to create more than 1800 retirement communities, each housing an average of 300 residents, according to Robert L. Schneider, an associate professor at Virginia Commonwealth University's School of Social Work. With the expectation of this kind of growth, developers have turned from the increasingly competitive and less profitable garden apartments to retirement homes, causing oversupply in some areas. Further, apartment developers have found those retirement complexes already built not that easy or profitable to manage. The transition from apartments to retirement units is complex, despite the profitable lure to serve a rapidly graying America.

Ultimately, the profitability will be there. In 1980, there were 2.2 million Americans over 85 and this group (the fastest growing in America) is expected to double by the year 2000. Moreover, the numbers are even greater for those over 75, when health problems usually force a change to a retirement community or nursing home. Thus, more retirement communities and nursing facilities must be built, which should generate growth estimated at 15 to 20 percent a year for years to come. Retirement communities range from simple rental operations to nursing homes with a wide range of services, including lifecare communities providing a broad choice of health, personal, and social services.

The market is not just in the sun belt. While areas such as Florida and Arizona have been well publicized for their weather and favorable tax climate, the majority of elderly people still stay in their own communities. Accordingly, opportunities for investing exist throughout the country. Lifecare centers are a specific type of retirement housing that caters to those who have not lived alone previously—widows and widowers, usually. A company with major stakes in the industry (and one that specializes in lifecare centers) is appropriately called *Life Care Services*. Within the past several years, this Des Moines, Iowa company has developed impressive management capabilities. Occupancy rates at its facilities are usually above 90 percent.

Among the other developers are Cardinal Industries, Charter Communities, and Forum Group. The latter builds and then transfers majority of ownership to limited partnerships, and operates a publicly traded company called *Forum Retirement Partnerships (FRL-ASE)*. However, we consider these companies speculative investments despite the significant, proven need for the services.

Over time, while a few exceptional operations will stand out, it is expected that the growth and profits will be captured by the major hotel operators such as Marriott, Hyatt, Holiday Corp., and Del E. Webb Corp. For example, Webb owns and develops retirement communities in Arizona including the well known Sun City West and Sun City Vistoso. They can handle the large capital costs with little difficulty. Further, their experience in site selection, housekeeping, food service, maintenance, and marketing is easily transferred to the retirement housing area. Conclusion: Retirement housing is a great growth area, but one in which there are few "pure plays" and where it is best to focus on experienced, well capitalized companies.

5

Hidden Assets: Sleeping Beauties Between the Balance Sheet

REAL ESTATE RICH COMPANIES

The dream of every investor is to find a company selling at a substantial discount from the real value of its assets. In recent years, enormous profits have been made through takeovers by individuals and groups that gain control of a company, then liquidate all or a portion of the company holdings at great profit to themselves and the remaining stockholders. Among some of the balance sheet items that command attention are assets under the categories of "land and improvements," "real estate," and "leases." Land and improvements is usually priced on the balance sheet at original cost, net of depreciation. Since land is not depreciable, it is valued at original cost, which valuation could be 20, 30, or more years old!

The attractiveness of raw land on the balance sheet reflects the operation of supply and demand. While the supply of usable land has remained unchanged, the demand from the nation's expanding cities continues to grow. In the past several decades, San Diego, Phoenix, and Orlando have exploded in terms of growth and rising land values, only to be superseded by Denver, Dallas, and Houston, which in turn were surpassed by Boston, Hartford, and Providence, Rhode Island! Growth in and around New York City has crossed the borders to southern Connecticut and the mid-New Jersey area, always at great profit to patient landholders. Long-term, relatively low-priced leases can also be valuable in such markets.

The question always arises: Why should these values exist? Aren't there literally thousands of sharp-eyed, sophisticated analysts searching for these bargain companies with undervalued assets? The answer is simple. One reason for Wall Street's overlooking value derives from the fact that sometimes mere size (a huge company) may obscure real worth, since that value may exist in one of the company's smaller component parts. Or, it could be related to a lack of available information reported on the subsidiary. For example, a real estate subsidiary or a subsidiary with real estate holdings could (and usually does because of accounting principles involved) report significantly lower net earnings. A case in point is McCormick & Co., a spice company, which has a sizable real estate holding in a subsidiary that is not consolidated with company operations. Further, where a company has a most complex capital structure, hidden value could lie in intricate corporate segments such as holding companies, partially owned affiliates, and majority-owned and minority-owned subsidiaries. The distinction between holding companies and operating companies is difficult for most investors. Throw in affiliates, subsidiaries, consolidated and unconsolidated, and the typical investor throws up his or her hands in despair and moves on to something easier. It is not the difficulty that repels investors but the patience and time needed to unravel the complexities. Yet, devoting a little time to developing an understanding (perhaps as much time as required for the viewing of a television movie) could yield profitable investment results. A good example of hidden value in intricate corporate holdings is Alexander's, Inc., a department store chain where there was value submerged in valuable leases revealed by a cursory review of balance sheets.

Finally, in addition to hidden real estate assets, there are also hidden earnings. More properly the term "hidden" should be replaced by "understated." Earnings understatement occurs because of the accounting convention associated with fixed assets. Fixed assets are depreciated or written off over a period of time. The writeoff is an amount each year that, when totaled, will cover worn out or obsolete assets, or, more likely, the maximum writeoff allowed under current tax law.

The base for figuring depreciation is the original price of the asset. While it may be true that trucks, aircraft, and machinery do lose value over time—they are either worn out from use or obsolete (as in the case, say, of a plane) because a new one is more efficient—this does not apply to a properly maintained building such as a warehouse or office building. Buildings usually appreciate rather than depreciate in value. Accordingly, where a company's earnings have a large segment of real estate depreciation, the result is understated earning power.

RAILROADS AND HIDDEN REAL ESTATE ASSETS

Before you can uncover hidden real estate value in stocks, you must first know what "value" is. *Webster's Dictionary* defines value as "the monetary worth of something." The stock market (really, the aggregate of all investors) defines value as the lower-than-the-market-average price paid for either earning power (present or future) or book value. Accordingly, when a stock's price is below "value" it becomes attractive. This variation between market price and intrinsic value is the basis for stock profits.

While obvious asset undervaluation is unusual except in bear markets, it does exist. The hidden asset value results from the public's lack of familiarity with a company. Obscurity shelters value in a real sense. An intricate corporate structure leads to undervaluation.

In the late winter and spring of 1987, railroad stocks began to inch their way up on Wall Street's price charts. Week after week stocks such as CSX and Burlington Northern moved up in price on rising volume. Was this because the economy was improving and rail traffic would soon be generating substantial revenues? Hardly! What investors were beginning to realize was that railroads were loaded with real estate values, which could be exploited by emphasizing development of commercial and industrial parks along the rail lines. Further, an industrial park adjacent to a railroad could increase the railroad's carloadings. Land development is a natural extension of the railroad business—one so rich with promise in certain cases that management is hiring or developing the necessary expertise.

Among real estate rich companies, railroads rank at the top of the list. The reason is simple and historical—more than a hundred years ago, the United States Government and some states made large land grants to fledgling railroad companies to provide for their rights-of-way. Since then much of the land not used for rail operations has risen in value dramatically but is still carried on the railroads' balance sheets, at value significantly below the market.

Most railroads own potentially valuable commercial and industrial development sites, usually carried on the books at the low costs incurred generations ago. Land in or near any major city is especially valuable. Once a railroad develops industrial parks, it can begin to develop multi-use sites—high-rise office buildings and office parks on the periphery. This converts land from a low cost asset to a highly valued one, resulting in significantly increased net income.

Obviously, in analyzing rail stocks for purchase as hidden asset-rich stocks, your analysis must begin with company operations in the basic business—rail traffic. Here volume and profitability are linked to the national economy as well as U.S. export markets. Further, you should check company or brokerage reports regarding a railroad's traffic mix. Autos are high-rate traffic; commodities are lower rated and afford lower profit margins. Additionally, the rise or fall of oil prices affects railroads significantly. For example, a rise in oil prices would have a threefold effect on rail companies:

1. it improves the railroad's competitive position versus truckers (for whom fuel is a larger percentage of cost);

2. it enhances the competitive position of coal, the rail industry's highest volume commodity; and

3. it increases revenues for the companies' oil and gas subsidiaries.

Among the companies that own significant, well located acreage are *Santa Fe (Southern Pacific Corporation [SFX-NYSE])*, *Union Pacific (UNP-NYSE)*, and *Burlington Northern (BNI-NYSE)*. Santa Fe Southern's real estate holdings are estimated to be worth some $5 billion! The company leases about 28,000 acres of commercial and industrial property and owns nearly 3 million acres of agricultural, grazing, and desert land.

Union Pacific has been a pioneer in value enhancement of its nonrail holdings. Burlington Northern has enormous mineral resources as well as undeveloped acreage. In the East, *Norfolk and Southern (NSC-NYSE)* is well worth a close look. It has a strong balance sheet and, historically, a most efficient operation. CSX is another eastern rail carrier that has attractive value possibilities. It was formed several years ago by the merger of Chesapeake and Ohio and Seaboard Coast Industries.

OTHER COMPANIES WITH REAL ESTATE INTERESTS

Perini Investment Properties, Inc. (PNV-ASE) is a Framingham, Massachusetts-based real estate company involved in the purchase, development, and operation of investment-type real estate. Among its holdings is a 6 percent interest in the prestigious ALCOA building in San Francisco, adjacent to the financial district.

Grubb and Ellis (GBE-NYSE) is the nation's largest publicly traded real estate firm. In the early 1980s the company purchased more than a dozen real estate-related businesses. The bulk of its revenue comes from commercial and industrial brokerage commissions. Significant penetration has been achieved in the West, particularly California. The company appears to be well positioned to profit from the growth of pension fund assets oriented toward real estate and foreign buyers. Among the major competitors are companies such as Cushman & Wakefield and Coldwell Banker, a subsidiary of Sears Roebuck.

Patten Corporation (PAT-OTC) is a major (if not the dominant) acquirer and seller of rural land to individuals in the northeastern and mid-Atlantic states. Operations are centered on acquiring large, underdeveloped rural properties within two to five hours of metropolitan areas, which are then subdivided into parcels averaging about 12 acres each. Sales are made mainly to metropolitan residents who seek to establish rural property ownership. Patten offers financing to purchasers. The company markets through more than 24 offices with heavy use of direct mail and newspaper advertising. Property inventory is turned over rapidly with the period from acquisition of acreage to its sale generally ranging from one to 12 weeks. The company has been public since November 1985.

"LAND RICH" COMPANIES

From the earliest moments of recorded history, land has been a major source of wealth. Like gold, it has always attracted investors; but unlike gold, its value persists because land is one of the most essential natural resources. Economists are fond of pointing out that there are four basic elements of production: land, labor, capital, and the entrepreneur who puts them all together. Land can be rented, developed, or left idle for later use. Another factor that commends land as a basic investment is the low management demand it places on the investor.

As cities grow, land in the path of development will increase in value. Towns rarely grow evenly in all directions. Further, favorable zoning is increasingly more difficult to get thereby enhancing the value of existing land that has already been zoned and improved.

An assortment of "land rich" companies is outlined in the next few pages.

Newhall Land & Farming (NHL-NYSE) is a diversified land resource company that operates farms and develops commercial and residential real estate property in California. Commercial properties are developed for income by NHL, and its homebuilding unit, Valencia Company, designs, constructs, and sells properties to others. The company owns more than 120,000 acres of land in the Sacramento and San Joaquin valleys.

The real estate and national economic cycles occasionally provide an opportunity to buy NHL at a distinct discount from real estate value. For example, in the Fall of 1981, NHL stock fell to a low of 12–1/2 (adjusted) because of anticipated poor earnings. Particularly hard hit were residential and industrial land sales, which were in a downturn because of the national recession. In point of fact, earnings per share did drop from the $1.17 recorded in 1981 to $.43 in 1982. But by the end of 1983, earnings had rebounded to $.70 a share and the stock had more than doubled from its low.

Of more intriguing interest is the acreage of land that each share of NHL controls. It provides a solid long-term asset cushion against the swings in operating earnings.

Tejon Ranch (TRC-ASE) owns the Tejon Ranch in California, the largest privately owned contiguous landholding in the state, with 270,000 acres located 60 miles north of Los Angeles. The company engages in alfalfa seed production, cattle raising, and leasing land for oil and mineral production. While TRC has continually stated it has no plans for any substantial commercial or residential development of its property, it is constantly monitored by Wall Street value hunters. Its huge land holdings so close to one of the largest (and fastest growing) metropolitan areas in the United States will always cause it to be the subject of rumor. As a result, the stock has been a volatile price performer over the past several years.

Chicago-Milwaukee (CHG-NYSE), a former railroad, went through a bankruptcy reorganization from 1977 to 1985 and emerged a healthy, land-rich company. Today it is a real estate holding company that owns 96 percent of CMC Real Estate, formerly the Minneapolis Railroad. In 1985, the company sold the railroad to the Soo Line, but retained ownership of over 63,000 acres of rail tracks. The company's valuable holdings include 948 acres of industrial sites and 33,700 acres of timberland in Washington state. The stock is an excellent investment for long-term investors seeking substantial capital appreciation.

New Mexico & Arizona Land (NZ-ASE) operates not only as a land and development company but has placed increasing emphasis on developing its uranium and oil and gas holdings. Nevertheless, the big attraction here is the enormous holdings of development acreage in New Mexico and Arizona. The company also has rights to oil, gas, and minerals on over 1 million acres. From time to time, the company has sold or swapped its land to improve its holdings or operational flexibility. For example, between 1984 and 1986, the company sold an Albuquerque, New Mexico hotel, a Flagstaff, Arizona apartment complex, and a 62-acre tract of land in Mesa, Arizona. During that same year, NZ exchanged a large block of land in northern Arizona for a smaller parcel in the greater Tucson area. During the same period, it bought a shopping center in Green Valley, Arizona for more than $10 million.

Alico, Inc. (ALCO-OTC) also bills itself as an agribusiness, primarily engaged in the production of citrus, cattle, and forest products with gross revenue derived from these combined sources ranging from 60 to 70 percent of total revenues. The company also engages in land rentals for farming, cattle grazing, recreational, oil exploration, and miscellaneous uses, with gross income from these sources in the last five years ranging from 1 to 6 percent of total revenues. Revenue from mining of rock, sand, and other road-building and construction material by independent operators on company lands is another important source of income, producing from 5 to 10 percent of total revenues. The real "gem" in this company's operations is its ownership of more than 182,000 acres, which include timberland, pasture, citrus, and other agricultural acreage, as well as land under development.

McCormick & Co. (MCCRK-OTC), well known manufacturer and distributor of spices, extracts, seasonings and convenience foods, is also substantially engaged in real estate through its unconsolidated subsidiary: McCormick Properties. McCormick Properties develops and operates commercial and industrial properties in Maryland, Pennsylvania, and Florida. Its most successful industrial park is Hunt Valley just north of Baltimore. Shares that are traded are nonvoting shares, of which institutions own almost half the total.

Alexander's Inc. (ALX-NYSE) is a striking example of a real estate-rich as opposed to a land-rich company with a primary focus in another line of business. Alexander's operates retail department stores located in metropolitan and suburban areas of New York City. Its real estate holdings include ownership of AAA property and long-term leases on superior locations—all carried on the books at levels far below fair market value. For years the real estate was an unrecognized part of the company's total value. One particularly valuable and highly visible property is on Lexington Avenue in Manhattan across from Bloomingdale's, one of the prized retail locations in New York and currently underutilized.

As late as 1982, the stock sold at a low of 7–1/2. However, in 1983 investors began slowly to perceive that the stock was selling at a low level even for its retail earnings, which were estimated at over $1.00 a share, up from $.71 the year before. At that point, the stock was selling at slightly under 10 times those estimated earnings. Nothing was being paid for the extraordinary real estate values the company owned. Investors began to flock to the stock on the assumption that the company would either have to begin developing its real estate potential or it would be taken over by investors eager to develop Alexander's prime properties. The result: In two years, Alexander's soared from a low of 9–3/4 to 43.

Zayre is a retailer operating a chain of discount stores. It owns an 82.5 percent interest in TJX Co., a discount apparel retailer the company spun off early in 1987. Zayre's underpriced real estate holdings, a combination of valuable leases and direct ownership, attracted significant attention from investors in late 1987, moving the stock from a low of about 22 to a high of 36 in only a few months.

6

Limited Partnerships: Big Deals for Small Investors

If you think tax reform took the bloom off real estate limited partnerships, read on. Tax reform tackled partnerships designed to create shelter, not income. Economically sound partnerships continue to prosper. At today's lower individual tax rates, income-oriented partnerships with moderate or no financing give investors attractive yields and good growth prospects. But, how can you separate the winners from the losers? Let's take a closer look at partnerships and find out.

WHAT IS A LIMITED PARTNERSHIP?

Basically, all limited partnerships have the same structure. The syndicator (sponsor) is the general partner and manager. Capital is raised by selling limited partnership units to individual investors, who become limited partners. They own a share of the partnership. In real estate limited partnerships, investors' liability is limited to the amount of money they invested.

The real estate partnership buys one or more income-producing properties. Income and tax deductions pass directly to the limited partners. In five to 10 years, the properties are usually either sold or refinanced and the profits distributed to the partners.

The critical element that separates economically sound partnerships from speculative syndications is the way the partnership invests the money raised from the limited partners. To fully appreciate this difference, and the importance of investing only in economically sound partnerships, you must understand the two basic types of partnerships and how they operated before tax reform. We shall also show you how they've revised their investment strategies to deliver deals with economic merit.

PARTNERSHIPS CAN BE PUBLIC OR PRIVATE

There are two types of real estate limited partnerships: public and private. Public partnerships are registered with the Securities & Exchange Commission (SEC) and state securities agencies. The offering is detailed in a lengthy report called the prospectus, which outlines the partnership's investment objectives, the syndicator's background, past performance of the sponsor's other partnerships, financial projections (if the properties have been selected), and the division of income and sales proceeds between the general and the limited partners. Public partnerships usually spread their risk by purchasing several properties.

The majority of limited partnerships are public. A typical partnership unit ranges in price from $2500 to $5000. Investors interested in using IRA and Keogh account funds can generally invest with a lower minimum, usually $1000 to $2000.

Even before tax reform, many public partnerships focused on deals with economic merit. Generally, they delivered a respectable quarterly dividend and offered modest tax shelter. Tax reform went after an entirely different type of limited partnership—those created primarily to generate tax shelter. Most of these were private partnerships.

Private partnerships are governed by the Securities & Exchange Commission's rule called Regulation D. It permits them to have an unlimited number of "qualified" investors (individuals with a minimum annual income of $200,000 for three years and a net worth of at least $1 million), plus up to 35 "nonqualified" investors.

Private partnerships are considerably more expensive than public partnerships and usually require staged pay-ins over a 5-year period. For example, investors buying into a partnership with a minimum $150,000 investment would make five annual installment payments of $30,000 each.

In this book, we will focus primarily on public partnerships. However, the investment guidelines we recommend apply to both public and private partnerships. Both share the common purpose of investing capital for the best possible return. For that reason, they both seek economically sound real estate investment.

YESTERDAY'S PARTNERSHIPS OFFERED TAX APPEAL

During the early 1980s, many private real estate limited partnerships, known as RELPs, made headlines by buying speculative, highly leveraged properties intended to provide huge tax write-offs for investors. Many RELPs had no economic merit. Their primary purpose was to create a tax shelter and future capital gains for affluent investors.

At that time, the tax laws permitted investors to use the substantial losses generated by RELPs to reduce their total tax liability. Partnership losses could be deducted from any type of income: salary, dividends, interest, royalties, rents, and so on.

More importantly, many private RELPs enabled investors to take tax writeoffs two or three times greater than their total investment. That was a particularly appealing benefit when the top Federal tax rate was 50 percent. (Before 1981, the top Federal tax rate was a whopping 70 percent.)

In an effort to reduce taxes, investors poured billions of dollars into RELPs designed solely to provide shelter. Since syndicators were selling losses—not real income—they could outbid traditional income-oriented investors like pension funds or wealthy private investors for almost any property.

As a result, many RELPs paid huge premiums to buy property for syndication. In the process they helped fuel speculation and overbuilding in many markets. At the same time, they cost the Federal government hundreds of millions of dollars in lost tax revenue by encouraging investors to deduct dollars they never spent. Most of the losses were generated through accrued interest deductions (investors deducted interest that was owed but not payable until a future date).

The combination of unhealthy speculation and paper losses for wealthy investors generated negative headlines from coast to coast. By the time Congress sat down to rewrite the tax laws, the aggressive behavior of many RELPs made them an obvious target for reform. Accordingly, Congress changed the rules. Suddenly, it was a whole new ball game.

TODAY'S PARTNERSHIPS: CASH IS KING

Tax reform nixed the shelter game for private partnerships. Congress classified real estate income and losses as "passive." Under the new law, passive losses can only offset passive income.

Today, partnership losses cannot be used to reduce "ordinary" (salary) income or "portfolio" (interest, dividends, royalties, etc.) income. However, excess losses aren't lost forever. You can carry unused passive losses forward indefinitely to offset passive income or sale profits in future years.

Tax reform forced syndicators to create RELPs that produce income. Shelter became a secondary benefit to offset current income and future gains. Today cash is king.

As a result, today's RELPs are income-oriented investments. The big change has been to no or low leverage. Syndicators buy property on an all-cash basis or with moderate leverage, financing only 40 to 60 percent of the purchase price. By eliminating mortgage payments, or holding them to a conservative level, the RELP enjoys a genuine cash flow.

Investors are the big winners. Now they get quarterly cash dividends, all or partially sheltered. In addition, they own part of an economically sound real estate investment with good capital appreciation potential. Today investors can make real money in real estate, and that's the name of the game.

ADVANTAGES OF A REAL ESTATE LIMITED PARTNERSHIP

You can buy real estate many ways on Wall Street, but only a RELP gives you the same economic benefits as buying property on your own. Unlike a corporation or a real estate investment trust (REIT), a RELP passes its income and losses directly through to the partners. Income is taxed only once—at the individual level. Losses can be used to offset partnership income or income from other passive investments. A RELP gives you many other advantages and conveniences, too, which include:

Current income. Today's income-oriented RELPs pay quarterly dividends (all or partially sheltered) on your investment. Most RELPs pay limited partners first; some even offer a minimum guaranteed return.

Tax benefits. All or a portion of your dividend is sheltered from taxes. The shelter comes from property depreciation and mortgage interest (if the RELP finances part of the purchase price of the property). Partnerships that pay all cash for property offer modest shelter; those that finance their properties offer moderate shelter. Of course, taxes are really only deferred. When the property is sold, taxes must be paid on the gain and the depreciated portion of the property.

If a mature RELP refinances appreciated property, the investors enjoy a tax-free cash distribution of the loan proceeds. However, refinancing rarely occurs before a RELP is five to seven years old. Those that buy property on an all-cash basis would be unlikely to change their investment strategy and incur unnecessary debt, while RELPs that finance a portion of their purchase price might well refinance the property later if it appreciates substantially.

Equity and appreciation. When you invest in a RELP today, you own a substantial equity position immediately. Partnerships that buy on an all-cash basis own 100 percent of the equity; RELPs that finance 40 percent to 60 percent of the purchase price still enjoy a healthy 40- to 60-percent equity position.

In addition, well located and professionally managed property will appreciate in value as the cash flow increases. This adds significant potential for capital appreciation when the property is sold.

Limited liability. Your liability is limited to the amount of money you invest. This benefit is important since most small investors must assume personal liability when they buy investment property individually.

Professional management. Your property is managed by experienced professionals with a proven track record for buying and managing major properties for maximum income and appreciation.

Affordable investments. You can buy into a good RELP with a minimum investment of $2500 to $5000 (IRA and Keogh account minimums range from $1000 to $2000). If you want to make a larger investment, you can buy more partnership units.

Partnerships are easy to purchase. Most major brokerage firms offer several different types of RELPs. You can choose from RELPs that buy property on an all-cash basis or finance a portion of the purchase price. You can also target your investment dollars by selecting a RELP that buys a specific type of property, such as apartments, shopping centers, office buildings, hotels, or self-storage units. You can review the promotional materials and prospectus in the convenience of your home or office. When you select one that matches your investment goals, you can complete the enclosed subscription agreement and return it by mail.

PARTNERSHIPS ARE LONG-TERM INVESTMENTS

Historically, RELPs have one drawback in the minds of most investors. They are not liquid investments. Most hold property five to 10 years before selling and distributing the profits to the partners. In reality, this is an advantage. Real estate is a long-term investment. If you sell too soon you forfeit the future appreciation that makes real estate a profitable, total return investment.

Fortunately, there is a growing market for the sale and purchase of "used" partnership units. In addition, some newly formed RELPs plan to list their partnership units for sale on one of the national stock exchanges. But, keep this point in mind: At present, RELPs should still be viewed as long-term investments. There is no guarantee that you can sell your unit if you need your money. Also, most used partnership units sell at a 25 to 30 percent discount to their initial price.

The best time to deal with the liquidity issue is before you invest in a RELP. Evaluate your total financial position, your current and future income prospects, your short- and long-term financial commitments. In addition, plan to set aside a comfortable cash cushion for unexpected expenses like emergency home repairs or uninsured medical expenses. This money should be kept in a stable liquid investment, like a money market fund or T-Bill account. If you are planning to buy a typical $5,000 partnership unit, ask yourself, "Can I afford to tie up my money for the next eight to twelve years?" If not, don't invest in a RELP.

On the other hand, if you are investing for your IRA or Keogh account ($1000 to $2000 minimum), time is on your side. If you're under 50, you won't be withdrawing money for another 10 to 15 years, so you can afford to make a good long-term investment. For information on where to sell a "used" partnership unit, see "Where To Sell a 'Used' Partnership Unit" later in this chapter.

LEVERAGE: FRIEND OR FOE?

In simple terms, leverage refers to borrowed funds. In real estate, that usually means mortgage financing.

If you buy a building for $100,000 and finance the purchase with a $70,000 mortgage, the deal is 70 percent leveraged.

Leverage lets you magnify your total return, or loss, on appreciated property. The difference between a leveraged purchase and an all-cash purchase is illustrated in the following charts.

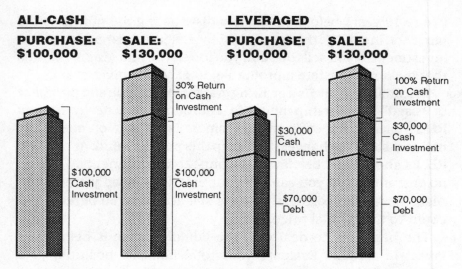

A building was purchased for $100,000 and sold for $130,000.

The all-cash purchase produced a $30,000 profit on a $100,000 investment—a 30 percent return to investors.

The leveraged purchase produced a $30,000 profit on a $30,000 investment financed with a $70,000 mortgage—a 100 percent return to investors.

Investors in the leveraged purchase earned over three times more than investors in the all-cash purchase.

Although leverage can double or triple your total return, it carries greater risk. For example, if the vacancy rate of the property rises, income from remaining tenants might be insufficient to pay the monthly mortgage and operating expense. In a worst-case scenario, the property could be foreclosed.

If you want the appreciation potential of leverage with a reasonable degree of safety, follow this investment formula. Buy into a moderately leveraged RELP that finances no more than 60 percent of the purchase price. Reduce your risk further by selecting a RELP that owns prime properties located in strong growth markets.

On the other hand, if your financial objectives are primarily safety and regular quarterly dividends, you'll probably be more comfortable in a RELP that buys property on an all-cash basis. In essence, you'll be trading the opportunity for substantial capital appreciation for more security and steady income. You'll still have a good opportunity for capital appreciation. It just won't be as great.

The decision to buy into a leveraged or an all-cash RELP is a matter of knowing your investment goals and matching them with your risk tolerance level. Then, pick the best RELP you can find in that category.

YOU CAN TARGET YOUR INVESTMENT DOLLARS

When you decide to invest in a limited partnership, you can put your money into the type of property you would like to own individually. For example, if you're bullish on the future of apartments, a number of reputable sponsors form partnerships that invest only in apartments; or you can select a partnership that buys only office buildings, shopping centers, self-storage units, hotels, or almost any other type of real estate.

There are two types of partnerships that are unique and deserve separate descriptions. They are vulture partnerships and mortgage loan partnerships.

VULTURE PARTNERSHIPS PREY ON PROBLEMS

If you're in the market for a super high risk investment that could really hit the jackpot, vulture partnerships may appeal to you. These partnerships buy financially distressed or mismanaged properties at bargain basement prices. Their goal is to turn those troubled properties into profitable, income-producing investments with a resale value far greater than their original cost.

Buying into a vulture partnership is not for the faint of heart. Your capital is at risk. You could lose every penny you invested. But if you win, you could win big—*very* BIG.

Don't expect immediate cash flow and income. Troubled properties are frequently located in weak markets. They usually have high vacancy rates. In fact, they may even be vacant when the partnership purchases them. It may be several years before the properties have enough tenants and income to pay dividends to the investors.

Furthermore, you'll need patience. It will take a good five to seven years, possibly longer, to get most of these troubled properties operating at their optimum level—the stage at which they will command a top sale price.

The most important asset a vulture partnership can have is a top-flight real estate developer as the sponsor. Troubled properties require experience, and lot of it. They need a hands-on developer who knows how to create value and manage for maximum efficiency. If you're going to take a flier in a vulture partnership, fly with a pro. It's the only way to go.

MORTGAGE PARTNERSHIPS FINANCE REAL ESTATE

Some limited partnerships buy mortgages, not real estate. They loan money to developers to buy existing income-producing property or to build a new project.

Mortgage partnerships are income-oriented investments that get the bulk of their income from interest payments. Some partnerships make participating mortgages that give them a percentage of cash flow and residual profits when the property is sold.

Although mortgage partnerships lack the appreciation potential associated with owning real estate, they can give you steady income at very attractive yields. Mortgage partnerships are relatively safe if they invest in existing properties that meet the following criteria:

1. the property is owned and managed by a developer with a successful track record;

2. the amount of the mortgage is 80 percent, or less, of the property's acquisition price;

3. the property is leased and generates sufficient cash flow to service debt and give the owners a respectable return on their equity (banks historically allow approximately 80 percent of cash flow for debt service);

4. the property is well located in a prosperous area of the country.

Financing new construction is always riskier than lending money on an existing property with good tenants and a stable cash flow. The level of risk rises or falls in relation to the amount of money loaned, the location of the project, and the developer's track record. Ideally, the partnership should not finance more than 75 percent of the construction cost.

The real trouble starts when partnerships finance property in problem areas of the country—areas that are either overbuilt or economically depressed. Projects in these areas typically lease up slowly. When that happens, the developer may not have enough income from the project to make the mortgage payments. In a worst-case scenario, the partnership might have to foreclose on the mortgage.

However, there are plenty of good investment opportunities available. In the next section we take a closer look at how to find them.

HOW TO FIND A QUALITY PARTNERSHIP

Locating a RELP that matches your investment goals requires some homework. Visit several brokerage firms in your area. Tell them what type of RELP you would like to buy. Be specific. For example: "I'm looking for a RELP that buys quality apartments on an all-cash basis. I want a syndicator with a strong track record and a deal that offers current dividends and good appreciation potential."

Don't get sidetracked by other RELPs the broker may be selling. They may be perfectly good deals but may not match your investment objectives. Know what you want. Be persistent until you find it.

Before you invest, keep these guidelines in mind:

1. **Invest through a reputable firm.** Deal only with established securities brokers or national syndicators with in-house marketing teams. You can often get good recommendations from reputable law and accounting firms. Beware of unsolic-

ited telephone offerings or cold calls from high-pressure salespeople.

2. **Review the syndicator's track record.** You want an experienced general partner with a proven track record of success owning and managing major properties. You'll find this information in the prospectus. Look in the table of contents for a section entitled "Prior Performance of the General Partner and Affiliates."

3. **Determine how income and profits will be shared.** What percentage of cash flow and profits goes to the limited partners and what percentage goes to the general partner? Good RELPs pay limited partners a specified rate of return first. The general partner doesn't share in any income or profits until the limited partners receive a return on invested capital.

4. **Look at the syndicator's fees.** Are they reasonable in relation to the services being provided? Keep in mind that all investments, including stocks and bonds, involve a sales commission. No one manages money free of charge; however, a growing number of syndicators defer their sales and marketing commissions until the property is sold and the partnership dissolved.

   The fee structure and profit sharing arrangements of partnerships are analyzed in *The Stanger Register.*[1] Stanger reduces the complex analysis to one number showing the investor's overall share of the pie. Stanger also rates limited partnerships (AAA, AA, B, etc.) to reflect safety of capital invested.

5. **Avoid highly leveraged RELPs.** They carry a greater risk and usually generate large tax losses. Chances are you won't be able to use the losses. In the post-tax reform climate, RELPs with more than a 70 percent debt-to-equity ratio carry a higher investment risk and the probability of generating more losses than you can currently use.

---

[1]For further information on this service, contact *The Stanger Register,* Robert A. Stanger & Co., L.P., 1129 Broad Street, Shrewsbury, NJ 07702-4314. Telephone: 201/389-3600.

6. **Look for all-cash or moderately leveraged RELPs.** Concentrate on income-oriented offerings. You want a RELP that pays you regular quarterly cash dividends and anticipates attractive appreciation potential.

7. **Avoid RELPs that finance property with zero-coupon mortgages.** These RELPs attract investors with higher yields achieved by deferring all mortgage payments until the loan is due. This gives the RELP more money to pay bigger dividends up front. But when the loan comes due, the accrued principal and interest usually wipes out all the equity and appreciation in the property.

8. **Weigh the risk-return ratio.** Remember the old rule of investment: The higher the risk, the higher the return. RELPs that pay all cash for property carry a lower risk. Accordingly, they pay a conservative dividend with good capital appreciation potential. A leveraged RELP carries more risk because it finances part of the property's purchase price. It has the added expense of mortgage payments. But it also has the opportunity to multiply its total return through the power of leverage. Consequently, leveraged RELPs pay slightly lower dividends, but they provide more tax shelter, and offer above-average appreciation potential.

TOO MANY PASSIVE LOSSES?

Tax reform trapped many investors in real estate partnerships designed to generate large passive losses with no passive income to offset them. Unlike previous tax bills, the provisions of the 1986 Tax Reform Act did not "grandfather" investors who bought partnerships to shelter income prior to 1986.

If you are caught in the passive income/passive loss crunch—and can't use all your passive losses—don't panic or rush out to make a quick investment that promises to generate passive income to offset your losses. Tax reform didn't wipe out excess passive losses immediately. They are phased out over a 5-year period.

Even if you don't have passive income, you can still deduct a

Table 6–1
Passive Loss Deduction Schedule

Tax Year	Percentage Deductible
1986	100% of any losses
1987	65% of any losses
1988	40% of any losses
1989	20% of any losses
1990	10% of any losses

percentage of your passive losses against ordinary income through 1990. Table 6–1 shows the deduction table Congress approved.

Any unused partnership losses can be carried forward indefinitely to offset future passive income and profits from existing or other passive investments. That can be a valuable deduction if your partnership has a sizable gain when the property is eventually sold.

Here's another tax-planning pointer. When you sell a limited partnership interest, you can deduct the accumulated passive losses against your ordinary income.

Here's why. The purpose of the passive income provision is to prohibit taxpayers from deducting passive losses before they are actually incurred. There is one proviso, however: You must sell your partnership interest to an unrelated party. Intrafamily sales or transfers won't cut the mustard with the Internal Revenue Service.

SHOULD YOU BUY A PASSIVE INCOME GENERATOR (PIG)?

Many private partnership investors faced with excess passive losses are rushing to buy investments known as passive income generators (PIGs). These are usually income-oriented RELPs that buy property on an all-cash basis.

Why are these investors attracted to PIGs? Income from PIGs can be sheltered by PALs (passive activity losses). In other words, these investors are buying passive income to offset their excess passive losses. Before mixing PIGs and PALs in your portfolio, ask yourself this question, "Can a PIG help my PAL?" Buying a PIG may be a quick solution to the medium-term aggravation of excess passive losses, but is it also a sound deployment of additional investment capital?

Let's assume you have $5000 in excess passive losses. If you want to buy a PIG to offset the losses immediately, you would have to make a substantial long-term investment that would tie up your capital eight to 12 years. Assume a typical PIG is yielding about 5 to 6 percent annually. Therefore, to generate $5000 in passive income, you would need to invest between $83,000 and $100,000.

Even if you can afford to put that much money into a long-term investment, you should consider the after-tax yield you could get from an alternative investment. Would you be ahead putting your money into a higher yielding liquid investment? Your income would be taxable, but at today's lower rates. Also, liquidity would let you switch investment strategies more easily in response to changing economic conditions.

You should also weigh the possibility that Congress could change the tax laws again. They have done so every year since 1981. They may very well tinker with tax reform to stimulate a sluggish economy or to encourage investment in a particular area.

No one knows when or how Congress will eventually alter existing tax laws. But one thing is certain. There will be future changes in response to economic and political issues. If they ever change or modify the passive income/loss regulations, investors who buy PIGs solely to offset losses could get caught with excess taxable income. And that income would be locked into a long-term investment.

The bottom line? Don't overreact to tax reform. Don't jump into quick solutions. They may be full of quicksand. Do evaluate your financial situation. Investigate all your investment options before making a decision. Above all else, keep this rule in mind: Every investment should make economic sense and should offer a realistic potential for profit. Successful investors always follow this rule. It consistently brings them profits—and helps them avoid losses—in all economic climates and through ever-changing tax laws.

WHERE TO SELL A "USED" PARTNERSHIP UNIT

Sometimes the best plans go awry. Circumstances change. Emergencies arise. Investors alter their goals. Fortunately, if you simply must cash out of a RELP, there is a growing resale market for "used" partnership units.

Start with the syndicator. Many keep a list of other partners who want to buy more units in the same partnership. If you bought your partnership unit through a securities firm, call your broker. Securities firms often have clients anxious to buy into existing limited partnerships with a successful track record.

If your sponsor or broker doesn't match buyers and sellers, or you'd like to get another bid, there is a growing number of firms you can contact. For further information, and a quote on the current resale price on a partnership unit, call or write any of the firms in the following list:

Equity Resource Group
1280 Massachusetts Avenue
Cambridge, MA 02138
617/876-4800

Liquidity Fund Investment Corporation
1900 Powell Street—Suite 730
Emeryville, CA 94608
800/633-9090 (outside California)
800/227-4688 (in California)

MacKenzie Securities
650 California Street
San Francisco, CA 94108
800/821-4252

National Partnership Exchange
100 West Kennedy Boulevard— Suite 260
P.O. Box 578
Tampa, FL 33601-0578
800/356-2739 (outside Florida)
800/336-2739 (in Florida)

Oppenheimer & Bigelow Management, Inc.
489 Fifth Avenue—Suite 3400
New York, NY 10017
800/431-7811

Partnership Securities Exchange
1814 Franklin Street—Suite 820
Oakland, CA 94612
415/763-5555

Private Securities Network, Inc.
145 Marina Blvd.
San Rafael, CA 94901
415/456-8825

Raymond James & Company
1400 66th Street North
St. Petersburg, FL 33710
800/282-8863 (outside Florida)
800/237-7591 (in Florida)

Realty Repurchase, Inc.
50 California Street, 13th Floor
San Francisco, CA 94111
800/233-7357 (outside California)
800/222-7357 (in California)

The bottom line: Limited partnerships provide an excellent opportunity for investors to own a share of investment-grade real estate. Quality partnerships have historically paid handsome dividends to limited partners. The key to finding profits in a partnership begins with careful homework. If you follow the rules outlined in this chapter you should be able to locate a partnership positioned for profit.

7

Master Limited Partnerships

Master limited partnerships became popular investment vehicles after Congress passed the 1986 Tax Reform Act. Sponsors claimed investors would enjoy the same tax benefits as traditional partnerships, avoid corporate taxes, pay higher yields than bonds, and give investors the liquidity of publicly traded stocks. Master limited partnerships were hot investments in early 1987.

Contrary to public perception, MLPs are not the progeny of tax reform. They had a fairly inauspicious arrival in 1978 when Tishman Realty and Construction rolled its real estate assets into Teeco Properties L.P., and finally gained public attention when Apache rolled up its oil and gas partnerships in 1981. But MLPs really took off after maverick Texas oilman T. Boone Pickens took over Mesa Petroleum. He reorganized the company into an MLP and garnered a reported $100 million on the deal.

Pickens' phenomenal success turned the Wall Street spotlight on MLPs. Everybody wanted to duplicate, or surpass, Pickens' record, and MLPs seemed like the perfect vehicle. Suddenly companies that didn't own a drop of oil saw an opportunity to circumvent corporate taxes by reorganizing as MLPs. The concept appealed to operating companies in fields as diverse as real estate, cable TV, fast-food restaurants, and grocery stores, to name just a few.

Real estate operating companies that generate ongoing income from rentals, sales, property management, and related services reorganized into MLPs. They include home builders, hotels, fast-food restaurant locations, nursing homes, shopping centers, and mortgage banking companies.

As operating companies and real estate syndicators rushed to reorganize as MLPs, the Treasury Department began to calculate the potential loss of corporate tax revenues. When MLP formation reached record levels in mid 1987, Treasury officials warned they were considering taxing all publicly traded MLPs as corporations. Finally Congress, fearful that more companies would follow this strategy to circumvent corporate taxes, ruled that all publicly traded MLPs would be taxed as corporations unless they generate at least 90 percent of their income from investments, real estate, or natural resources. Their dividends would be classified as portfolio income and could not be used to shelter passive losses.

Despite their altered tax status, carefully chosen MLPs may present sound investment opportunities for investors. Their principal advantage over traditional limited partnerships is liquidity. Since they may be taxed as corporations, they should be analyzed as corporate stocks for investment purposes.

MLPs COME IN THREE VARIETIES

When you go shopping for an MLP, keep in mind that MLPs can be structured several ways.

"Roll-out" MLPs

When corporations want to tap the equity in their real estate assets, they may sell part of their real estate assets to investors through a "roll-out" MLP. If the corporation owns valuable real estate, it may be more economical and profitable for the corporation to sell the real estate and lease it back. This strategy can release millions of untapped dollars for continued growth and development.

Burger King utilized this technique in February, 1986, when it spun off its nationwide Burger King locations into the Burger King Investors MLP. As the owner of AAA fast-food locations, the MLP gets a base rent plus a percentage of gross sales at each location.

Since "roll-out" MLPs usually have all their eggs in one basket (like fast foods, nursing homes, hotels, etc.), they are slightly riskier than MLPs that own diversified operating companies. However, if the MLP owns assets leased and managed by a successful company in a monopolistic or growth industry, it may be an attractive investment.

"Roll-in" Partnerships

"Roll-in" MLPs usually buy and manage real estate for maximum cash flow and appreciation. Roll-ins are structured to permit the sponsor to offer new units (similar to a stock underwriting) to raise capital to buy more investment real estate.

"Roll-up" Partnerships

"Roll-ups" are formed by combining several existing real estate limited partnerships into a new MLP. Sometimes the sponsor mixes troubled partnerships with stronger ones to lower the overall operating costs and make the weaker properties more profitable. Because roll-ups often contain property from troubled partnerships, they generally carry greater risk than other types of MLPs. Investors should examine roll-ups carefully to see if they include weak properties and whether the new MLP can perform profitably.

MLPs OFFER THREE REAL ESTATE PLAYS

There are three ways to participate in the real estate market via MLPs: (1) income property MLPs; (2) mortgage loan MLPs; and (3) real estate-based operating business MLPs. Each offers a different type of real estate investment. A summary of their activities and a listing of the major MLPs in each category follows.

Income Property MLPs

These MLPs own one or more properties. Investor return is based upon the income generated by the real estate. These MLPs offer more of a traditional real estate play than MLPs that own real estate-based operating businesses. The latter's income fluctuates with the fortunes of a particular industry, while an income property MLP does not. Its ability to generate a healthy cash flow—and an attractive return—is dependent upon the same factors that influence other investment real estate. MLPs in this category include Cal Fed Income Partnership, L.P., Gould Investors L.P., Newhall Investment Properties, U.S. Realty, and The Marina.

In addition, three MLPs concentrate on regional shopping centers: Equitable Real Estate Shopping Centers (Minnesota/ Michigan), EQK Green Acres L.P. (Long Island), and Shopco Laurel (Maryland).

The largest income property MLP is American Real Estate Partners, Ltd. American owns a diversified portfolio of over 300 properties rolled up from 13 partnerships originally sponsored by Integrated Resources.

Mortgage Loan MLPs

Among the several choices you have in this market, you can choose an MLP that offers a fixed rate of return. For added safety, select one with a government or independently insured mortgage program. Currently traded MLPs in this area include: American Insured Mortgage Investors, Winthrop Insured, and American First Federally Guaranteed Funds.

If you want steady income plus upside potential, and are willing to accept a slightly higher degree of risk, consider participating mortgage MLPs. These partnerships share in the property's income above a certain level so your rate of return grows as the property prospers and appreciates. MLPs that make participating mortgage loans include American First Tax Exempt Mortgage Funds I and II and Retirement Living Tax Exempt Mortgage Fund Limited Partnership. Although most mortgage MLPs generate ordinary income, these two give you tax-free income.

Real Estate-Based Operating Business MLPs

These partnerships provide you with a business investment coupled with a real estate play. These MLPs fall into six categories:

1. **Real estate developers.** These are primarily single-family home developers. They include NV Ryan, Interstate General, UDC-Universal Development, and Standard Pacific. Your return rides on the developer's product, marketing, and regional demographics, as well as interest rate swings that affect the homebuilding business.

    Other developers now operating as MLPs include Newhall Land and Farming and Universal Medical Buildings. Newhall develops commercial, industrial, and residential property on 123,000 acres near Los Angeles, while Universal focuses exclusively on designing and building medical facilities.

2. **Real estate services.** Three areas dominate this category: brokerage firms, mortgage banking, and property management.

    In the area of brokerage, Merrill Lynch rolled out its real estate subsidiary into Fine Homes International. Commonwealth Mortgage provides mortgage banking services, and Servicemaster provides commercial property maintenance.

3. **Retirement and nursing care centers.** The major MLPs in this area are Angell Care, Forum Retirement Partners, and National Healthcorp.

4. **Hotels and motels.** These businesses depend upon rising room rates and increased occupancy to boost cash flow and yield. These MLPs include Aircoa, Allstar Inns, LaQuinta

Motel, Pickett Suite, Prime Motor Inns, and Red Lion. Another MLP, Sahara Casino, combines the hotel and casino businesses.

5. **Restaurants.** These include fast-food franchises as well as more traditional restaurants. Restaurants can be risky businesses. They are subject to intense competition, changing consumer preferences, and economic cycles that affect disposable income.

   Early leaders include Burger King, Winchells Donut Houses, Perkins Restaurants, and USA Cafes (franchisers of Bonanza restaurants).

6. **Amusement parks.** These businesses are subject to more ups and downs than a roller-coaster ride: seasonal appeal, new competition, and general economic conditions. If you're in the mood for a little adventure, investigate Cedar Fair, L.P., operators of two amusement parks.

THE PROS AND CONS OF BUYING MLPs

To help you decide if MLPs are compatible with your investment goals, we offer here a summary of the pros and cons of owning them.

The Advantages of MLPs

1. **MLPs are liquid investments.** You can buy or sell them any day of the week.

2. **MLPs offer a wide range of investment choices.** Some MLPs own and operate real estate. Others are operating companies with a real estate-related angle such as casino hotels, nursing homes, fast-food franchises, and so forth.

The Disadvantages of MLPs

1. **MLPs trade on yield, not asset value.** Investors buy MLPs on the basis of yield, similar to buying bonds or other fixed-

income securities. The price does not reflect the underlying value of the real estate assets, however valuable.

This is a big negative for real estate investors. The bond-like behavior of MLPs effectively eliminates any real opportunity for capital appreciation—the big equity kicker in any good real estate investment. As a result, most existing real estate MLPs now trade at up to 20 percent below their original offering price.

Obviously, if you plan to buy a real estate MLP, you should wait until it proves itself in the market—that is, until the price has a chance to stabilize relative to other yield-oriented investments. Let the early birds swallow the market discount between underlying asset value and trading price.

2. **MLP prices can fluctuate.** Since MLPs are liquid investments that trade on the stock market, they are vulnerable to the same market swings that affect all publicly traded stocks. A bullish or bearish market can increase or decrease their trading price regardless of the MLPs' performance. Traditional partnerships, which are basically illiquid investments, are not subject to the same price fluctuations.

3. **MLPs don't return your principal.** When you buy a bond you get regular interest payments plus the face value of the bond back on the due date. Unlike bonds, MLPs don't return the principal you invested. This is why they typically pay higher yields than bonds.

Guidelines for Buying An MLP

1. **Don't buy the yield.** Although MLPs trade on yield, they aren't bonds; they don't return your capital. Thus, they are not a comparable investment with bonds.

2. **Buy the cash flow.** MLPs own an equity position in real estate or an operating company with income-producing assets. Concentrate on the cash flow. Look for MLPs with good prospects for increasing their cash flow.

3. **Buy MLPs with quality assets and favorable business prospects.** These factors are critical to the MLP's ability to consis-

tently deliver a high yield. For example, MLPs that own or operate real estate should control prime properties in AAA locations in robust economic markets. If the MLP owns an operating company, like a homebuilder or hotels, examine the current and future business prospects for that industry and area of the country.

4. **Look for strong management.** Invest only with proven professionals. The sponsor should have a successful track record owning and managing the type of property the MLP will own.

5. **Avoid MLPs financed with zero-coupon mortgages.** As we explain in Chapter 8, zero-coupon mortgages let the partnership pay higher yields by deferring mortgage payments until a future date—often seven to 10 years away. When the mortgage (plus accrued interest) is due, the partnership will pay it through a sale or refinancing of the partnership's property.

   In fact, this strategy could wipe out all your equity and appreciation—the major incentives for buying real estate. Exceptionally high yields always come with a tradeoff. In MLPs financed with zero-coupon mortgages you could be putting tomorrow's profits in your pocket today. If you do, there may not be any money in the till at the end of the deal.

HOW MLPs COMPARE WITH LIMITED PARTNERSHIPS

Investors who once shied away from limited partnerships because of their limited liquidity are now leaping into MLPs because they are a liquid real estate investment. However, as with any investment, all benefits have tradeoffs. The liquidity of MLPs carries a price tag. Following are the primary tradeoffs in buying an MLP versus a traditional limited partnership and how they can affect your yield.

1. **Price.** Because MLPs are liquid, they tend to trade on yield. This may not reflect the full value of the underlying asset. In

addition, since the MLP has an indefinite life, investors may never recognize the true asset value of the underlying investment.

If you buy a traditional partnership and hold it until it is liquidated in seven to 10 years, you will get the full value of the underlying assets. Of course, if you sell a traditional partnership prior to liquidation, you will generally have to discount the value 25 to 30 percent. Therefore, you should buy a traditional partnership only if you plan to hold it until liquidation.

2. **Current yield.** Although MLPs and traditional partnerships may have similar acquisition and operating costs, MLPs usually pay a much higher current yield. They must do this to attract investors and maintain an active market in their stock.

    However, in order to offer a significantly higher yield than untraded partnerships, many MLPs employ some form of "yield enhancement." For example, they may finance property with zero-coupon mortgages. By deferring payments of principal and interest until a future date, the MLP has more cash to pay higher dividends in the near and medium term.

3. **Interest rate risk.** Since MLPs tend to trade on yield, the price won't reflect improved performances by the MLP. For example, if you buy an MLP yielding 9 percent, and improved performance boosts payouts to a 12 percent yield, you would expect the price of your shares to rise. Not necessarily so. If interest rates rose several points during the same period, your MLP shares might be trading at your purchase price. If they were still yielding 8 percent, they would sell at a discount. On the other hand, if interest rates fell and you owned the high yielding shares, you should be able to sell them at a handsome profit.

4. **Return of capital.** Traditional limited partnerships give investors a full return of capital and a prorata share of capital gains when the property is sold, plus dividends paid during the life of the partnership. Master limited partnerships do not return the investor's capital; that is why they typically pay higher dividends.

5.   **Market timing.** When you own shares in an MLP, you must decide when to buy and sell. You must constantly assess all the economic and market variables that can affect the price of your investment. Traditional partnerships don't require ongoing decisions. They are a long-term investment. Ultimately, the general partner decides when the market will bring the best price for the real estate in the partnership's portfolio. The general partner sells, liquidates the partnership, and distributes the proceeds to the limited partners. Traditional partnerships are a truly passive investment that requires no decision from the investor.

WHERE TO GET MORE INFORMATION ON MLPs

If you would like more information on MLPs, contact your stockbroker or:

Investment Partnership Association
1050 Connecticut Avenue, N.W.
Washington, D.C. 20036
202/429–6578

For a list of publicly traded MLPs, see Appendix G.

8

Making Money in Mortgages

When you buy mortgages on Wall Street, you are really financing homes on Main Street. More importantly, you have a partner in the deal: Uncle Sam. The U.S. government guarantees the timely payment of principal and interest on every mortgage.

What do you get for your money? A high-yielding liquid investment that gives you steady income with a government guarantee. If that sounds too good to be true, keep in mind that the government guarantees the principal and interest payments, but the yield fluctuates with market interest rates. Since mortgages are interest-rate sensitive, they trade like bonds. There's the risk.

We'll explain this in greater detail as we examine the many different ways you can buy mortgages on Wall Street. At the same time, we'll show you how to minimize the risk for maximum income and preservation of capital.

But first, let's see exactly how mortgages move from Main Street to Wall Street. To understand how a mortgage on the house next door could end up in your investment portfolio, we'll watch your neighbors—the Browns—buy a home.

The process begins when your local bank gives the Browns an FHA or VA mortgage on their new home. The bank puts the

Browns' mortgage, along with many others, into a package called a "mortgage pool."

Next, the banker submits the mortgage pool to the Government National Mortgage Association (GNMA or Ginnie Mae), for approval. Upon acceptance by Ginnie Mae, who guarantees the timely payment of principal and interest to investors, the banker sells the mortgage pool to a securities broker.

At this point, the securities broker sells the Ginnie Mae mortgage-backed securities (MBS) to mutual funds, institutional investors, or individuals. Now it's the investors (you could be one of them) who own the mortgage on the Browns' home.

MORTGAGES COME IN AFFORDABLE DENOMINATIONS

For many years, Ginnie Mae MBS were purchased almost exclusively by pension funds and wealthy individuals. The minimum investment was $25,000, putting Ginnie Maes beyond the means of most investors. Finally, Wall Street divided larger Ginnie Mae certificates into $1000 denominations called "unit trusts." Soon mutual funds took the same route, giving investors a piece of the mortgage market for a modest minimum investment.

GINNIE MAES ATTRACT INTEREST

Once Ginnie Maes became affordable, their popularity soared. Investors snapped them up for their high yields and unique double Federal guarantee.

Ginnie Maes are guaranteed two ways. First, the underlying mortgages are insured by the FHA or guaranteed by the VA or Farmers Home Administration. Second, the Ginnie Mae certificates are guaranteed for the timely payment of principal and interest by the full faith and credit of the U.S. government.

In addition, Ginnie Maes are liquid and easy to purchase. Many major sponsors advertise Ginnie Maes in the newspapers and magazines. One quick call to a toll-free number brings their prospectus to your mailbox. Brokerage firms also sell Ginnie Maes.

GINNIE MAES TRADE LIKE BONDS

Those high yields that attract investors to Ginnie Maes can fluctuate. The yields quoted assume a pool of 30-year mortgages will be repaid in 12 years as owners sell or refinance their homes.

During periods of stable interest rates, Ginnie Maes give investors exactly what they bargained for. But when interest rates make a significant move upward or downward, investors find themselves in a new ball game, because Ginnie Maes trade like bonds. Their value moves in the opposite direction of interest rates. When interest rates rise, Ginnie Maes decline in value and sell at a discount.

Why does this happen and how can you maximize your gains and reduce your risk? When interest rates fall more than two points, homeowners typically refinance their mortgages at lower rates. Since they repay only face value (loan balance) of their mortgage, you must reinvest your capital in a market paying lower yields. This is known as the "prepayment risk" associated with mortgage-backed securities.

The greatest risk associated with prepayment is the potential loss of capital. If you sell your MBS at a lower yield than the yield at which you purchased it, you will lose part of your principal. On the positive side, if you sell your MBS investment at a higher yield than you purchased it, you will get more money than you invested, because other investors will pay a "premium" for the yield you are selling.

The key to making money in mortgage-backed securities is to buy high and sell higher. You do this by investing in high-yield MBS. Pocket the interest as long as mortgage interest rates remain high.

Monitor interest rates closely. As soon as mortgage interest rates fall 1–1/2 to 2 percent sell your MBS. There is not a significant prepayment risk on a 1–1/2 to 2 percent decline in the prime rate, because the costs of refinancing usually exceed the savings unless rates fall 3 percent or more. Those costs include the loan origination fee, points charged by the lender, and local recording fees.

Take your profit on MBS in the early stages of a downward move in interest rates. If you wait for a significant drop in rates, you risk loss of capital because the market value of your security will eventually decline.

HOW TO BUY GINNIE MAES

There are three ways to buy Ginnie Mae mortgage-backed securities.

Mutual Funds

Ginnie Mae mutual funds buy a diversified portfolio of mortgage-backed securities and sell shares in them to individual investors. Professional management and portfolio diversification help reduce the risk of untimely prepayments and fluctuating yields.

Mutual funds make mortgage-backed securities affordable by allowing investors to buy into the pot for only a few dollars a share. In addition, investors can have their dividends automatically reinvested in more shares of the fund.

For a list of Ginnie Mae mutual funds, see Appendix H. For your convenience, we've divided them into "no-load" and "load" categories and included the name, address, and telephone of the sponsor. A telephone call or letter from you will bring their prospectus to your home or office.

As with any investment, review the information carefully before you invest; if you have questions, call the sponsor. Most have toll-free telephone numbers. A reputable sponsor is always willing to answer legitimate questions, or clarify confusing points, for current or potential investors.

Unit Trusts

Unlike Ginnie Mae mutual funds, which actively trade mortgage-backed securities, unit trusts own a fixed portfolio of securities. They put all their eggs in one basket.

Owning a fixed portfolio of securities makes unit trusts more vulnerable to market interest rates. If rates rise, the underlying value of the portfolio will decline and investors will see their capital erode.

If interest rates remain steady, or decline, unit trust investors will own golden eggs. Steady interest rates will give them continued high monthly income. Declining rates will boost the value of securities in their portfolio, creating capital appreciation in addition to the already attractive income.

Unit trusts come in affordable denominations, starting with a minimum investment of $1000.

Ginnie Mae Certificates

If your primary objective is safe, steady income and you have at least $25,000 to invest, your best bet is an individual Ginnie Mae certificate. These certificates are popular with retirees seeking the security of a regular check each month. Since they buy the certificates for the income, and usually hold them to maturity, they get all of their capital back.

When you own an individual Ginnie Mae certificate, the amount of your monthly check allocated to principal and interest changes each month. This is an accounting headache, because the interest portion of your check is taxable income and the principal is not taxable since it is a return of capital—the money you invested when you bought the certificate. When you own an individual certificate, you don't have the dividend reinvestment option available with a mutual fund. However, this gives you a steady stream of money to deploy into another investment opportunity.

Now we take a look at an investment that gives you the benefits of Ginnie Mae MBS and eliminates nearly all of the prepayment risk.

MORTGAGE BONDS: HIGH YIELDS, LOWER RISK

The best way to get the benefits of Ginnie Mae MBS and substantially reduce the risk of fluctuating yields is to buy mortgage bonds called CMOs (collateralized mortgage obligations). CMOs were created expressly to insulate investors from the prepayment risk associated with Ginnie Mae MBS.

The basic difference between Ginnie Mae MBS and CMOs is this: Investors in MBS own a share of the underlying mortgages; MBS are a direct obligation of the U.S. government. Investors in CMOs own bonds backed by Ginnie Mae certificates and the underlying mortgages.

Collateralized mortgage obligations substantially reduce your risk by giving you a high level of protection against mortgage prepayments. They usually do this by dividing the bonds into four separate maturity classes: A, B, C, and Z. Each bond class has a different interest rate and maturity date. The bonds are typically retired by their maturity dates (two, five, 10, and 20 years).

Income from the mortgages, including any mortgage prepayments, is always used first to pay the interest and retire the bonds with the shortest maturity. Class A bonds are fully retired at the end of two years, then income from the mortgages is assigned to pay interest on and retire Class B bonds, and so on.

The CMO strategy of always applying mortgage payments against the bonds with the shortest maturity stabilizes the yield, especially in Class C and Z bonds, because Class A and B bonds are paid off first. As a result, you normally get the original yield for the full term of the bond you select.

Collateralized mortgage obligations yield about 2.5 percent more than Treasury securities of the same maturity and carry an AAA credit rating from Standard & Poor's and Moody's. They carry the same Federal guarantee as Ginnie Mae MBS. They are available from securities brokers, are liquid, and are sold in denominations of $1000.

The face value of your CMOs is subject to the same market risk as a Ginnie Mae MBS certificate or other bonds. That means if you want to sell your bond prior to maturity, it would sell at a premium or a discount, depending upon current interest rates.

In addition to CMOs, another type of mortgage bond luring investors into the market is called a real estate mortgage investment conduit (REMIC). As with CMOs, these bonds are paid off sequentially, helping to stabilize the yield and protect the investor's capital.

The primary difference between a CMO and a REMIC is the quality of the underlying assets. Typically, CMOs finance quality real estate that assures them an AAA rating by Moody's and Standard & Poor's. A REMIC, on the other hand, can be collateralized by any type of property—including financially distressed real estate. In reality, some REMICs are "junk" mortgage bonds.

Because of the greater risk associated with junk bonds, you must get complete details before investing in any REMIC. It will be fairly easy to spot offerings of junk mortgage bonds. Just look for a deal that offers an exceptionally high yield comparable to other mortgage bonds. The higher yield is a red flag for you to take a much closer look. When you dig deeper, the chances are 99 out of 100 you'll find a junk mortgage bond.

Despite the higher risk, junk mortgage bonds may still be a good investment. The critical factors to consider are the location of the property and the track record of the owner. If the REMIC is collateralized by well located property being purchased by a strong developer with a top track record, both the property and the mortgage bond could be big winners.

FANNIE MAE: SWEETER YIELDS, HIGHER RISK

Ginnie Mae's "sister," Fannie Mae (Federal National Mortgage Association), buys pools of residential mortgages not insured or guaranteed by any agency of the federal government. They are known as "conventional mortgages."

Although Fannie Mae is not a household name on Main Street, it's a powerhouse on Wall Street. The publicly traded company (FdNM-NYSE) is the third largest corporation in the United States, with an average trading volume of more than 500,000 shares per day. It holds assets of approximately $100 billion.

As the nation's largest private investor in home mortgages, Fannie Mae began issuing mortgage-backed securities in 1981. In less than five years, Fannie Mae MBS topped $100 billion—the fastest growth of any mortgage security in history.

Initially, Fannie Mae MBS were sold in large denominations to institutional investors in America and abroad. In the mid-1980s, Fannie Mae expanded its MBS program to individual investors by offering certificates in minimum denominations of $1000 each.

Fannie Mae guarantees the timely payment of principal and interest on each certificate regardless of whether the homeowner actually makes his mortgage payment. The guarantee is made solely by Fannie Mae—not by the government.

The advantage of investing in Fannie Mae MBS is the higher yield. Since Fannie Mae MBS do not carry the Federal guarantee associated with Ginnie Mae MBS or Treasury obligations, they generally sell at a higher yield. The absence of a Federal guarantee is not considered a significant risk factor since Fannie Mae, the nation's third largest corporation in terms of assets, is a substantial guarantor.

The yield on Fannie Mae MBS is subject to the same market fluctuations as the Ginnie Mae MBS. Your actual yield will depend upon the prepayment rate of the mortgages in the pool underlying your Fannie Mae certificate. Also, since mortgage-backed securities trade like bonds, if you sell your certificate prior to maturity, the market value of your certificate could be higher or lower than the face value, depending upon prevailing market conditions.

Fannie Mae MBS are bought and sold through stockbrokers. Larger brokerage firms are linked to an established secondary trading market for Fannie Mae MBS. This is an important point to consider before you invest. Since you might want to sell your MBS before maturity, you should only purchase MBS through a brokerage firm that actively trades them.

Your broker should be able to give you all the information you need to decide if Fannie Mae MBS meet your investment portfolio needs. If you would like more information, you can contact Fannie Mae directly at:

Director of MBS Investor Marketing—Fannie Mae
3900 Wisconsin Avenue, N.W.
Washington, D.C. 20016-2800
202/537-6628

ZERO-COUPON MORTGAGES: HIGH CURRENT INCOME

Zero-coupon mortgages are a new and creative method of financing investment real estate. Their principal appeal is a higher yield for both lender and borrower. Here's how they work: The lender foregoes the usual monthly payments of principal and interest in return for a lump sum payment of principal and compound interest in the future. The mortgage is typically due in about 10 years.

Real estate investors and developers like to buy property financed with a zero-coupon mortgage because they get a substantially higher current return. By deferring the mortgage payments, their current yield is around 4–1/2 to 5 percent more than financing the property with a conventional mortgage and about 3 percent higher than if they paid all cash for the property.

Lenders like zero-coupon mortgages because they receive a higher yield to compensate them for the lack of an immediate return. However, as with zero-coupon bonds, these mortgages carry imputed taxable interest each year. That means the investor must pay tax on income he won't receive for years. For this reason, zero-coupon mortgages are most popular with tax-exempt retirement accounts, including IRAs and Keoghs.

Zero-coupon mortgages carry other risks, too. Since there is no secondary trading market, it may be difficult or impossible to sell a zero coupon before maturity. But a greater risk is the possibility that the property owner may not have enough money to pay off the mortgage when it becomes due. For that reason, it is important to invest in zero-coupon mortgages that finance only experienced developers acquiring prime properties. Look at the track record of the borrower and the economic feasibility of the real estate project.

Although zero-coupon mortgages carry a greater degree of risk, they can be a good investment for high current income. If you want to have your cake and eat it too, you've got to do your homework carefully. You can reduce your risk by following these guidelines:

1. **Invest with an experienced sponsor.** Assessing real estate risk and growth potential takes professional skills. Look for a sponsor with a proven track record of buying and managing investment property profitably.

2. **Examine the debt-to-equity ratios.** The mortgage, plus accumulated interest, should not exceed 80 percent of the property's acquisition price. This ratio leaves a cash cushion of 20 percent—plus appreciation—to pay off the mortgage when it is due through a sale of the property or a mortgage refinancing.

3. **Finance only existing properties.** Don't buy zero-coupon mortgages used to finance property that will be constructed. Put your money on an existing project with a proven track record for attracting quality tenants and generating a healthy cash flow each year.

4. **Don't finance vulture funds.** They invest in troubled property, like empty office buildings in hard-hit Houston. These are highly speculative deals. Financing them with zero-coupon mortgages is like buying compound risk.

You can get such information on specific zero-coupon mortgages from the prospectus, or you can ask your broker to get the answers for you. To save time, your best bet is to ask your broker for the information and the page reference to it in the prospectus, then verify the information just to be sure there is no misunderstanding.

Don't invest until you're satisfied you have found a quality mortgage. And don't invest in zero-coupons at all unless you have a fairly high risk tolerance level. Even under optimum circumstances, these mortgages put your capital at risk, so don't be seduced by the high yields. If you can't live with risk, you can't live with zero-coupon mortgages.

MORTGAGE BANKING COMPANIES

Another way to make money in mortgages is to buy the stock of profitable mortgage banking and financial service companies.

These institutions make money by giving mortgages to home buyers and then servicing the loans they originated.

Mortgage bankers make money two ways. First, they earn money on the spread between their cost-of-funds and the income on their loan portfolios. Second, they make money servicing the loans they originate; they retain a small percentage of each monthly payment of principal and interest they collect for the owner.

Mortgage banking, like homebuilding, is a cyclical business. It is particularly sensitive to rising interest rates.

In addition, it carries the risk of "regional exposure" for institutions that make the majority of their mortgages in a particular geographic area. For example, lenders with large mortgage portfolios in the southwest have been hit with record foreclosures as the oil crisis has put thousands of residents out of work in Texas, Louisiana, and Oklahoma.

Although mortgage banking was originally a regional business, it is rapidly shifting to a handful of major financial service companies that lend nationwide. The regional mortgage banker who needs 45 days to issue a mortgage commitment can't compete profitably with financial conglomerates that make conditional loan commitments in 48 hours backed by billions of dollars in assets.

The following companies are rapidly increasing their market share of this lucrative market:

Chase Bank—CMB-NYSE

Citicorp—CCI-NYSE

Ford Motor Credit Corp.—F-NYSE

General Motors Acceptance Corp.—GM-NYSE

Green Tree Acceptance—GNT-NYSE

Lomas & Nettleton Mortgage Corp—LMC-NYSE

Primerica—PM-NYSE

Sears Mortgage Corporation—S-NYSE

Wells Fargo—WFC-NYSE

Weyerhauser—WY-NYSE

Of course, as we indicated earlier in this chapter, the Federal National Mortgage Association (Fannie Mae) is the largest owner of residential mortgages in America. It does not originate mortgage loans—it buys them on the secondary mortgage market. Fannie Mae stock is publicly traded on the New York Stock Exchange (FdNM).

9

How To Analyze a Stock Like a Pro

Selecting stocks that go up is not easy, but it is not impossible either. The key to successful stock selection requires careful analysis and decision making based upon facts—not emotions. Confusion arises from contemplating the various strategies that experts employ to make money in the stock market. Such methods range from buying stocks that are "cheap" on a book value or a price-earnings basis (buy low/sell high) to the opposite end of the spectrum: Buy stocks in companies that are growing fast and hitting new highs; then hope to sell them for big gains.

Then, there is the quality school of investing, which believes great quality in stocks is like great quality in precious stones or paintings: If you buy the best, you cannot go wrong. Still another school believes a stock hitting new highs is a good indication that you're buying the best; and on a technical basis, it means everyone who has bought the stock has a profit so there is no overhead resistance. This particular approach can be summarized as the "buy high/sell higher" school.

Actually, if you were to survey the strategies of top achievers on Wall Street, such as John Templeton and the late T. Rowe Price, you would find that they employ a variety of factors to sift out interesting stocks from the thousands available for further investigation.

The problem for most individual investors is how to compete with the near-geniuses like Templeton who buy and sell with the aid of high speed computers and a squad of analysts.

ESTABLISH SELECTION CRITERIA

First, you must have a clear understanding of the characteristics that successful stocks possess. Then you can use these characteristics to search for stocks with strong income and growth potential. Further, you must try to discover these winners at the early stages of their growth. You don't necessarily want to buy these stocks at the beginning of a move, but you want to invest early enough so a significant profit potential exists.

To most, the key to successful investing boils down to research, lots of hard work, and patience. If you assume that the existing market price of a stock reasonably reflects the prospects of that company in any point in time, then successful investors must dig deeper and further than most to extract the handful of "gems" that will outperform the rest. Some of the companies are difficult to analyze because of complex balance sheets or widely diversified operations, and these should be avoided. Also avoid highly cyclical stocks whose revenues and earnings have fluctuated widely over the past few years. Here you are competing with major investors who will be attempting to time the market. They seek to buy those volatile stocks when they seem cheap and sell them when they believe the price is too dear. The results are highly unpredictable.

Now that you know what *not* to buy, you are ready to start your search for factors that will clue you in to profitable stocks. One way to approach this is to ask yourself, "What makes stocks go up or down?" The obvious answer is supply and demand. If the demand for stocks is higher than the supply, the trend is up. But who puts the market up? Can we identify those buys? The answer can be found in the *Wall Street Journal* every day: The major buyers of stocks are institutions. About three-quarters of the daily trading on the New York Stock Exchange is institutional—buyers such as pension and profit sharing funds, investment advisors, and mutual funds. In the over-the-counter market, institutional buying is less pervasive, but it is still well above 60 percent of the total activity. So if you want to win on Wall Street you have to know the way institutions think, what they will *buy* and what they are likely to *sell*.

Several years ago a major public relations firm surveyed more than 1400 money managers, the *crème de la crème* of Wall Street's institutional establishment, to determine what major factors they considered in their stock selection. Surprisingly, the two most often quoted criteria were relative price–earnings ratios and earnings per share (both present and projected).

Amazingly, most professionals had little to say about company products, services, or management as factors in their selection. One reason for this may be that products or services are difficult to judge or measure in their early stages—when it counts! Once their products or services are successful they are clearly observable (and measurable) in the company's statistics. They felt management aptitude was too difficult to measure. Accordingly, since earnings and price-earnings ratios are of the highest importance, they are examined in detail.

EARNINGS PER SHARE

Corporate earnings, present and projected, are the most analyzed and emphasized financial criteria on Wall Street. A rising earnings trend is essential to any advance in a stock price. Even the conservative and legendary disciple of value investing, Benjamin Graham, knew that stock market success begins with the search for earnings and earning power. Graham noted that stock prices very quickly reflect any significant changes in either current earnings or Wall Street's perception of future earnings.

Your focus should be threefold: past earnings, current earnings, and projected earnings. Of these three factors, projected earnings are the most difficult to determine. Usually, the projection is a combination of past performance and consideration of any new factors that may affect that trend. Usually, the figure is available from analysts in the major stockbrokerage houses who cover the industry and the particular stock in question. Your local stockbroker or account representative can be helpful in providing this information.

One final point on earnings. The focus should be on earnings per share, not total earnings, since you can only buy earnings per share in the stock market.

PRICE-EARNINGS MULTIPLE

One of the keystones of investment analysis is the price you pay for earnings. This is the price per share related to the earnings, usually current earnings. If a stock is selling at $15 and has earned $1 per share over the past 12 months, the P/E multiple is 15.

You can even apply this multiple to the stock market as a whole. One gauge of the market is the Dow-Jones Industrial Average of 30 stocks. Another more widely used indicator is the Standard & Poor's 500. You can get the P/E of the market by taking the combined earnings (per share) of the S&P 500 and dividing it into the price of the 500 average. The resulting figure gives you the valuation of the market. But does it?

The bull market of the 1980s occurred, at least initially, in the face of declining earnings. Yet, earnings are usually regarded as the engine that leads equity prices higher. In 1985, the Standard & Poor's 500-stock index showed a total return, or market appreciation plus reinvested dividends, of 31.79 percent. Amazingly, the profits of companies comprising this index fell by an estimated 11.3 percent!

What moved stocks up was a sharp expansion in their price-earnings ratios. This expansion in earnings multiples was a direct function of a continued decline in interest rates. That's why price-earnings ratios are almost as important as earnings. The point is that the major bull markets usually are generated by either expanding price-earnings ratios or rapidly rising earnings. Ultimately, of course, for a bull market to continue, the decline in interest rates is replaced by a surge in corporate profits.

The same principle applies to stock prices. Initially, a stock moves up (following the market because of a decline in interest rates). But soon that price momentum must be justified by significantly higher earnings.

And now we come to the problem with price–earnings ratios: Which earnings are we talking about? The most common earnings are those of the 12 months—the so-called "trailing" earnings. This is the figure quoted in the daily financial column. But that "trailing" 12 months is history. Stocks don't sell on the past. They sell on investors' expectations of future earnings. These future earnings are projected by Wall Street analysts and portfolio managers.

In addition to the confusion over past and future P/E, we have the question of a standard of measurement in order to determine value. A price–earnings ratio of eight times earnings could be said to be low. But "low" in relationship to what? The REIT industry? The industry group would be one standard—comparing the P/E of one REIT to the average REIT multiple. Another method of comparison would be to use the stock market standard as another peg of value; in this case the S&P 500 average P/E.

What we now have is a matrix of value:

First—The Company P/E

Trailing 12 months

This year's estimate

Next year's estimate

Second—The Comparisons

Average of REITs or other real estate stocks

Trailing 12 months

This year's estimate

Next year's estimate

The price–earnings multiple varies from industry to industry (REITs for example), in terms of what investors are willing to pay for current and future earnings-per-share growth. The higher and more predictable the growth, the higher the P/E. The game for the investor is to seek the highest possible earnings growth at the lowest possible price. Lowest possible price translates to a stock selling below the P/E average of the industry or that of the S&P 500 with a higher growth rate than either of these standards.

Real estate is essentially a cyclical industry and therein lies a caution. Most experts will tell you that you should view P/E differently when looking at cyclical industries. In effect you should turn the rules upside down: buy when earnings are low, which usually makes for a high P/E. Investing in a "down" period will allow you to benefit when the upswing occurs. Conversely a low P/E hints the stock price is at the cycle's peak, ready for a fall.

Note too that P/E can be misleading when companies are recording losses. In the 1970s, REITs showed high P/E because their earnings were low but their potential was substantial. A better way to look at depressed firms is to compare price–sales ratios (stock price divided by revenue per share).

The P/E may be less relevant with companies that are valued chiefly by their assets, among which are real estate and oil companies and media companies whose main asset is dominance in a local market. Such organizations are often evaluated in terms of cash flow instead of P/E.

Price–earnings ratios are useful, but you must use them as the starting—never the end—point. While the search for low multiple growth is difficult, it is well worth the effort. To understand this, you must have a grasp on the dynamics of how stocks appreciate. Big price movements in stock come not only from higher earnings per share but also from increase in the price investors are willing to pay for these earnings. This dynamic duo of rising earnings and a rising P/E can be dynamite in capital appreciation. Put another way, big capital gains come not only from company growth but also from investors paying more for each dollar of that growth. A classic example is the almost legendary appreciation of the price of Bristol Myers (the major drug company) in the mid-1950s to mid-1960s. In the 10-year period from 1955 through 1964, earnings per share increased from $.50 a share to $2.18 per share, or an increase of 229 percent, as shown in Table 9–1.

But as the earnings kept on rising, investors became more impressed with that relentless growth. As a consequence, the

Table 9–1
Bristol Myers' Earnings Per Share, 1955–1964

Year	Earnings Per Share
1955	$ .50
1956	.59
1957	.68
1958	.73
1959	.85
1960	1.03
1961	1.23
1962	1.53
1963	1.81
1964	2.18

price–earnings ratio moved from 10 to 32. That was an increase of 200 percent, but the stock price rocketed from $5 a share in 1955 when earnings per share were $.50 and the P/E was 10 to $69 a share in 1964 when earnings were $2.18 per share and the P/E was 32! Incredibly, over a 10-year period, an earnings increase of slightly more than 300 percent produced a 1300 percent increase in price, the result of the dynamic duo of rising profits and a rising price–earnings ratio!

What we want is a company that is increasing its earnings per share by *at least* 10 percent a year. A company that is increasing earnings at 10 percent a year will double its earnings in a little over seven years. If the price–earnings ratio remains the same, the price of the stock will also double in seven years. But as we have seen, companies that have a consistent record of year-by-year growth become increasingly attractive to investors. The P/E begins to go up, which means the stock will probably double in considerably less than seven years.

Since the price you pay for earnings growth is important, the price–earnings multiple is a critical factor in stock selection. There is another way to reflect this relationship—in what is called the "earnings yield." This is the percentage of what the company earns each year based on the price you pay for it. For example, you buy a stock at $20 with earnings per share of $2, the P/E ratio is 10

Table 9–2
Earnings Yield

P/E	Earnings Yield
50x	2%
7	14.0
6	16.6
5	20.0
4	25.0
3	33.0
2	50.0

to 1. But an even more meaningful figure is the reciprocal, which is derived by dividing the P/E ratio into 100. That gives you the earnings yield. Table 9–2 shows how this really works.

Yes, this does mean that in a stock selling at seven times earnings, you are earning 14 percent. If the company paid all its earnings, you would get 14 percent! However, as a practical matter that won't happen. What does happen is that the earnings less dividends will be plowed back into the company to earn still more. As those earnings rise because of the plowback, the price of the stock should begin to reflect this growth. That is simple significance of earnings yield—it gives us clear, understandable numbers that express the relationship between price and value. Now when you see that 7x multiple, think of it in terms of earning 14 percent on your investment! The higher the earnings yield, the better.

THE SCORECARD

With two of the critical factors in stock selection developed, the next step is to isolate those companies that fit the criteria. There are over 420 real estate or real estate-oriented companies whose securities are traded on the listed stock exchanges or in the over-the-counter market. Out of this huge total the problem is to find those dozen or so stocks that have the best potential in terms of income, capital gains, or both. The problem seems enormous:

How does an investor sift through the data of all these companies and select just a handful? Surprisingly, it can be done—and done effectively—by any investor willing to devote a few hours a week to the discipline of sorting through the available material and making a few very basic calculations. For this we use a quick and easy approach called the stock selection scorecard.

THE STOCK CHECKLIST

We have summarized most of the quantifiable factors to use in your stock selection into two scorecards—one for finding growth real estate stocks and one for income real estate stocks. Filling out the scorecards should enable you to quickly accept or reject potential candidates for investment with a minimum of time and energy. You will need some simple tools, such as a current newspaper listing the latest prices, dividend information, high and low prices for the stock, and so on.

In addition, you will need to consult your broker or a good financial newsletter to get estimated earnings for your stock as well as that for the S&P 500. The inflation rate, as measured by the Consumer Price Index figure, can be found in a few minutes by checking with your local library, or again, your broker. (See how helpful a stockbroker can be?)

Checklist: Growth Real Estate Investments

Fill in the following items of information for use in your company file and scorecard computation.

Name of Company *(Symbol and Where Traded)*   _____
Latest Price   _____
52-Week Price Range (High & Low)   _____
Current Dividend   _____
Dividend Yield (yield divided by latest price)   _____
This Year's Estimated E/P/S   _____
Last Year's E/P/S   _____
Next Year's Estimated E/P/S   _____

Scorecard Computation   **Points**

1. *Next Year's Earnings Growth Rate*

    If E/P/S increase next year is estimated at *twice* the estimated inflation rate (measured by the Consumer Price Index), add four points; if between 50 and 100 percent of the CPI, add two points; if less than 5 percent, add zero   _____

2. *Past Three Years' Growth Rate in E/P/S*

    If annualized E/P/S growth over the past three years has been twice the annualized consumer price index growth rate, add four points; if between 50 and 100 percent of the CPI add two points; if less than 5 percent add zero   _____

3. *Earnings Trend*

    If earnings per share were up for each of the past five years, add four points; if earnings up for four of the last five years, add two points; if earnings were down in two of the last five years, subtract one point   _____

4. *Price Range*

    Is the stock selling at the low end of its 52-week price range? If yes, add four points; if price is midway between the high and the low of the year, add two; if at the high end of its price range, add zero   _____

5. *Price–Earnings Ratio Valuation*

    If the stock's current price–earnings ratio is less than the S&P 500 current price–earnings ratio, add four points; if it is nearly equal, add two points; if the stock's P/E ratio is 10 percent or higher than the current S&P 500 ratio, add zero _____

                                          Total _____

If the total score is 12 points or more, you have a potential growth stock on your hands.

Checklist: Income Real Estate Investments

Fill in the following items of information for use in your company file and scorecard computation.

Name of Company   _____

Latest Price   _____

52-Week Price Range (High & Low)   _____

Current Dividend   _____

Dividend Yield   _____

Current Year's Dividend   _____

This Year's Estimated E/P/S   _____

Next Year's Estimated E/P/S   _____

Scorecard Computation   **Points**

1. *Dividend Yield*

   If dividends are 100 percent higher than Dow Jones Industrial Average yield, add four points. Between 75 to 100 percent, add two points. For less than 75 percent, add zero   _____

2. *Past Three-Year Growth Rate (E/P/S annualized)*

   If more than 10 percent, add four points; 5 to 10 percent growth, add two points; less than 5 percent growth, add zero   _____

3. *Dividends Increases in the Past Three Years*

   If three times, add four points. If twice, add two points. If none, add zero   _____

4. *Price Range*

   Is the stock selling at the low end of its 52-week price range? If yes, add four points. If price is midway between the high and low of the year, add two; if at the high end of its price range, add zero   _____

Scorecard Computation continued   **Points**

5. *Earnings Growth*

    If fiscal earnings per share this year are expected
    to increase over last year and next fiscal year's
    earnings are expected to be up, add four points.
    If earnings this year are estimated to be up over
    last year, but it is uncertain or negative about
    earnings increases next year, add two points.
    Otherwise, add zero   _____

                                            Total _____

A score of 12 or more points indicates that this is a promising
income stock that should be investigated further.

Some additional comments on income real estate investment
for the scorecard: While a higher-than-average yield is an essential starting point for income-oriented investors, that yield (dividend) must be secure. Accordingly, your company selection
should have financial strength. One way for nonprofessionals to
check on this quickly is to use the Standard & Poor's *Earnings and
Dividend Ranking for Common Stocks*, usually available through
your broker or local library. Your stock, if it is rated, should carry
a B+ (average) or better. Additionally, dividends should have
increased over time. The history of dividend increases can be
checked readily through either company or brokerage sources.
We have used a 3-year time frame for dividend measurement; but
obviously the longer the record, the better. Further, since dividend increases depend on earnings increases, you should review
the earnings record to determine past trends as an indication of
what to expect in the future. Here again, while a 3-year record is
reflected in the scorecard, a longer record is most desirable. Once
you have decided *which* stocks have interesting investment potential, you have to determine *when* to buy. Many people translate
this into buying only when the stock market is "cheap" or "right."
This presumes that the stock is predictable.

WHEN TO BUY

Remember that we are seeking stocks with a profit potential over the next year to 18 months. The question is: Do we buy immediately or wait and watch? Many experts will advise that you should not invest if the market is too high, but rather should wait for better prices! Then these experts proceed to list a number of economic and financial statistics that will enable you to gauge the temperature of the market. Many believe the market is predictable and moves in cycles, and that a study of these cycles can yield improved timing, not only in buying an attractive stock but buying it in a down or declining market.

THE STOCK MARKET—PREDICTABLE?

The stock market cycle—a bull market that turns into a bear market—when observed from the distance of history, does seem predictable. One of the benchmarks to indicate the stock market's age is the way certain stock groups tend to repeat the past. For example, at the beginning of a market advance, the dominant investors are institutions, which tend to invest in large capitalization stocks, generally the issues of Fortune 500 companies. As the bull market matures, individual investors become more active and smaller stocks begin to attract more interest. The final stage of a bull market is characterized by the rapid appreciation of small stocks. According to cycle watchers, the best strategy seems to be to watch the movement of the blue chips during the first part of a bull market and, when smaller growth stocks start to rise in price, be ready to reduce your stock exposure. When the speculative frenzy is rampant, and tiny, unknown companies are rushing initial public offerings to market, that's the final stage!

Unfortunately, in point of fact, the stock market at critical turning points is highly unpredictable. Trying to relate past cycles to the present is nearly impossible. Accordingly, timing the market is not a productive use of time for most investors. The better way to determine when to buy is to watch the momentum of the market.

MOMENTUM

A stock in motion will continue in motion until confronted by an equal and opposing force. That statement smacks more of the physics laboratory than the stock market, and yet the law of inertia in physics can be applied successfully to stock selection. A stock may begin to move up (or down) in price for fundamental reasons, but after that initial move it begins to attract attention. If a stock is rising, potential and current investors gain more and more confidence in its ability to continue rising. Previous "fence sitters" regarding the stock will be compelled to quickly recheck their fundamentals and probably buy.

Further, technicians observing the pattern of increasing buying will proclaim that the chart pattern on the stock is favorable. This will excite even further buying. The logic is this: A stock that displays better-than-average strength possesses high probabilities of continuing that strength in the future. The reverse is also true. Weak stocks tend to continue performing worse than average. Again, our standard of measurement is the S&P 500 and the related real estate group of the stock in question.

Momentum, then, is important not only in determining *when* to buy, but also *what* to buy. After you have considered all other factors, you then look to see if the stock has been going up. If it has, then this is a strong recommendation to buy. If it hasn't gone up, but rather has been going down, the wisest course is to keep tracking the stock. When it stops going down and starts to go up, then you buy. Declining stocks usually take a long time to bottom-out and reverse their field. You don't want to buy them until they stop going down. Your time and money are too precious to be involved in a declining or at best sterile investment.

The late Gerald Loeb, one of the most successful stockbrokers of all time, who made millions in the tough markets of the Great Depression as well as the post-World-War-II era, was fond of repeating the point that the only reason for buying stock is that it is rising in price. To him, momentum was the single most important factor in purchasing a stock for profit. He emphasized that, time after time, he saw the tendency of established trends to continue. In his view (and ours), buying low and selling high is fine, but buying stocks that are rising and selling them at even higher prices is much safer and better.

RELATIVE STRENGTH

While momentum is an important indicator since it reflects a stock's trend, another factor of nearly equal importance is relative strength. This is the speed at which a stock is moving. A stock may go up 10 percent, which is satisfying in the short term, but it doesn't mean much unless you have a standard to measure the significance of such a 10 percent advance. If, for example, the stock market as reflected by the Standard & Poor's 500 went up 20 percent, that 10 percent advance isn't much. Accordingly, we measure a stock's performance by comparing it against an overall market indicator—either the Dow Jones or the Standard & Poor's 500. Usually, the latter is our favored point of comparison.

Specifically relative strength is gauged by the ratio of the stock's closing price to closing price of the market average. This can be done on an average price basis as well as a closing price basis, and on a daily or weekly basis. We prefer to do it once a week at closing prices since it is easier, and detail is not as important as trend. A month's results may look like the example shown in Table 9–3.

The conclusion we are led to is that our stock is falling behind—its relative strength is less than that of the market.

Table 9–3
Closing Price Ratios

	Weeks			
	1	2	3	4
Stock A	20	20 1/2	21	21 1/4
Market S&P 500	315	322	345	366

DIVERSIFICATION

We now have our stock(s) selected and have determined this is the time to buy. Remember that our time frame is more than one year, and we are looking for big gains. We have also done a great deal of work, so that any payoff should be big. By this, we mean: Don't underweight or, as Mark Twain noted, "Put all of your eggs in one basket—and watch that basket!" Twain's strategy was to concentrate—make the payoff really count. It also means that the losses can count as strongly—on the downside.

Diversification is an essentially defensive strategy aimed at protecting your capital by distributing it to various stocks. However, too much diversification can give you a lot of protection, but not much in the way of appreciation. Remember, we don't want to lose, but we are also in this game to *build* capital, not simply preserve it. The same rule applies to your time—too much diversification equals too many stocks and that can dissipate your energies and attention span.

Putting most of your eggs in one basket is not the same as owning one egg. In investing in real estate stocks, you should spread your money around among companies. Certainly the focus should be on REITs since they represent a larger and broader variety of real estate opportunities. Consider other companies such as Rouse and Trizec, and mutual funds and limited partnerships as well.

Also, don't forget that you can diversify functionally among REITs. For example, you can select a stock whose focus is on shopping centers, one on office buildings and so on. You can also diversify geographically. Remember, too, that the trick is to balance risk versus reward.

When all is said and done, and you buy that stock or stocks, the next and final step is to sell. Again the question: *When?* As Monte Gordon, Director of Research of the Dreyfus Funds, is fond of saying: "Buying is easy . . . it's like a romance with great expectations; but selling is tougher. Whether you own a winner or loser, breaking up is hard to do." Selling is difficult because it means either parting with a stock that has done well or, in the case of a loser, it means admitting that you were wrong. The road to profit is to be objective and unemotional about your investment decision from the very beginning. You must have a clearcut sell discipline in place when you buy the stock. The easiest sell disciplines are: (1) a predetermined sales price at which you are willing to sell; and (2) sell when you've made a mistake in the original purchase and it becomes increasingly clear that the company's prospects are less favorable than you originally believed.

An example of selling at a predetermined future price would be the case of buying a stock at $20 per share believing it could go to $45 a share over the next 12 to 18 months. You should write that future sales price in your stock record book with a note as to why you bought the stock. That note should include some of the details of the stock's attractiveness, or you can substitute P/E for a stock's price as a sales target. Let's say you buy a stock with a P/E of 8 and the stock's price–earnings relationship moves it to a P/E of 12. Then assume further that the market multiple (the S&P 500) is 11. You might choose a selling point using the rule that when a stock reaches or exceeds the market multiple, it is no longer a value.

The second discipline is to sell when you've made *a mistake in the original purchase* and it becomes increasingly clear that the company's prospects are less favorable than you originally believed. Here you must refer to those notes you made when you bought the stock. Are the underlying fundamentals of the company deteriorating? Does it look permanent? Did you buy the stock because earnings rose 15 percent last year? If you did, and earnings begin to slip—growth at only 5 percent for two quarters—then it looks like that 15 percent rise won't be attainable this year. Usually, when something goes wrong in the fundamentals, it lasts a lot longer than people expect. You should sell, or at least review your reasons for purchase again.

Finally, what if the stock starts to go down for no apparent reason? Say you bought the stock at 20; and, instead of going to 45, it begins to drop to 18 . . . then 17 . . . and then 16! What do you do? Well, if the overall market is down, your stock is just acting normally. But what if the stock market is flat or up? Call your broker, yes. Check with the company, too. Perhaps both checks are positive. Then you've got to make the hard decision. Here again you must set in advance a price at which you will sell at a loss. Some investors use as a rule of thumb a 10 percent decline, after which it's an automatic "out." We view that margin for error as too tight. A more usable automatic sell signal would be a 15 percent decline. After that, sell no matter what the explanation from the company or your broker.

If professional investors agree on anything it is this: Take your losses quickly. A small 10 or 15 percent loss has a tendency to become a horrible 25 or 30 percent loss all too soon. We might add that you can't afford too many 15 percent losses in your portfolio, either. Those 15 percents add up, and deplete assets very fast!

One way to minimize your overall losses is to try to learn something from each losing experience. Review each investment purchase and sale decision with care to determine what, if any, error of judgment occurred.

Finally, if a stock doesn't make much price progress for a period of time—say a year—you might consider selling simply on the basis of inaction. Time is money, in your work and in the stock market. If a reasonable time has elapsed, yet the stock still appears to have the same attractive fundamentals that led to your purchase, it may be difficult to kick it out. Nevertheless, you should look around for a more attractive investment. When you find it, sell out that dull stock.

More times than not your sale will be frustratingly wrong, at least temporarily. If the stock goes up you will grit your teeth and say: "I knew that stock would go higher." Forget it! Stick to your discipline. If you sold at a profit yet missed an even bigger profit, take heart! You made a nice gain and that is the whole purpose of investing. You probably will not get the last point of profit, ever.

If you sell and then the stock rebounds, grit your teeth, stick to your discipline and admit that at times you will be wrong. Never look back! There are lots of other stocks around.

Let's review the process. We have carefully screened out of hundreds of potential investment possibilities a few stocks. We have determined these are the stocks to buy and we have further decided that *now* is the time to buy.

WRAPPING IT ALL UP: THE FINAL OVERVIEW

Here is a simple checklist to enhance the probability of your making it in the stock market: A magic "seven," if you will:

First and foremost, the one successful strategy that has made money in good times and bad is to buy stocks of well capitalized companies at lower-than-market multiples. If you simply relegated your stock selection to those companies rated B+ and above by Standard & Poor's, you would save yourself a lot of grief early. These stocks usually do better than average.

Second, if you invest in small companies look for quality, not speculative, ventures. Focus on companies with significant growth potential, strong management with a stake in the company, and access to capital markets. Remember, institutions *are* the market. We want stocks the institutions will want to buy eventually, so buy what *they* are likely to buy—hopefully before the big crowd runs the price up. Remember, too, that this means lots of small attractive companies will be passed over, and they will tempt you with their outstanding values. Leave them alone. Let them stay undiscovered. Major brokerage houses cannot afford to have their expensive research staffs identify and analyze small companies, since it is not what they consider cost effective. What they are looking for are companies with enough outstanding stock so that when they make a recommendation, their brokers can buy (or sell) lots of stocks and generate commissions. This factor guides us to our potential and limited universe.

Certainly, small company investing has a place—for the very patient. But it may take years before these companies grow to sufficient size to tempt Wall Street attention. In the meantime, the small stock investors may be happy with their values, but with precious little market action to enrich their portfolios. If you insist on doing this for a greater reward, that is fine—but the risks are greater too. Nevertheless, there are some rules here: Look for a good track record and an expanding share of the market, but also remember that small stock investing is hard, grueling, and for long periods of time, not very satisfying work. The average investor who lacks persistence and patience should still stick with rules one and two.

Third, stay away from "concept themes" and tips. While it may be nice and flattering to be the beneficiary of some "hot" and supposedly inside information, you should always ask yourself, "Why are these people being so good to me?!"

Fourth, check the price of the stock versus its yearly high and low. Usually a stock selling at its high will stall and decline a bit, giving you a better buying opportunity later. As for top stocks selling at their lows, be wary. Wait until they go up a bit before buying.

Fifth, stock research coverage is important for monitoring company progress as well as attracting new buyers. Be sure there are brokerage houses that follow your stock and regularly comment on its progress.

Sixth, historic price–earnings ratios are useful in terms of perspective. You want to know what has been the highest and lowest P/E ratio of your stock with the average of the Dow 30 and the S&P 500.

Seventh, and last, beware of unconventional accounting. You don't have to be an expert to determine the source of a company's earnings gains. If most of the increases come from regular operations, that's fine. Watch out for nonoperating earnings, which is where the accounting tricks are played.

10
Mind Over Money

Why do some investors hit so many home runs while others just keep striking out?

Research indicates winners on Wall Street share a positive psychological attitude that allows them to exercise maximum control over their actions and emotions in managing their money. In addition, they share another five winning characteristics:

1. A well defined game plan;
2. Realistic investment objectives;
3. Confidence to resist the "herd instinct" that fuels most trading on Wall Street.
4. The patience to stay in cash until they find the right investment and the patience to give a good investment time to ripen to its full profit potential;
5. The ability to learn from their mistakes and turn those lessons into future profits.

Let's take a closer look at these characteristics and see how you can put them to work developing and managing your investment portfolio.

A WELL DEFINED GAME PLAN

A successful trip to Wall Street begins with a well defined game plan. You need to know exactly what you want to achieve. To succeed you must develop a prudent game plan.

It is not enough to say, "I want to make some money." Who doesn't? You must be specific. How much money? Over what period of time? How much can you invest each year?

Without carefully chosen goals, and a realistic plan to reach them, you'll end up with a hodgepodge of impulse investments. If you earn an attractive total return on your money with this strategy, send a dozen red roses to Lady Luck.

Buying and selling stock on a hit-and-miss basis is like instructing an airline pilot to fly from New York to London with the directions, "Head east."

REALISTIC INVESTMENT OBJECTIVES

Most investors move into the stock market with a nebulous goal: to make lots of money. It is a nebulous goal because real money—profit—is always measured in percentages, not dollars.

The irony of this investment approach pops up in conversations every day. There's the friend who says, "I sold Park Place Properties this morning and made $5000. Isn't that great?"

It depends. How much capital did he invest (put at risk)? How long did he hold the stock? What was the *total return* on his investment?

If his return was 8 percent and he could have made 9 percent in T-Bills or CDs (with no risk), it was a lousy investment. If he earned 15 percent in the same market, it was excellent. Too many people set out to make a killing in the market, nearly getting slaughtered themselves, because they have no clear sense of direction for achieving a realistic balance between risk and return.

For some reason, they think they have to double or triple their money overnight to build an attractive nest egg.

Actually, most people could achieve handsome rewards by concentrating on a total annual return on cash invested of 15

Table 10–1
Investment Gain Based on 15 Percent Annual Return*

Cash Invested	20 Years	30 Years
$ 5,000	$ 81,832.50	$ 331,058.50
10,000	163,665.00	662,117.00
15,000	245,497.50	993,175.50
20,000	327,330.00	1,324,234.00
25,000	409,162.50	1,655,292.50
50,000	818,325.00	3,310,585.00
100,000	1,636,650.00	6,621,170.00

*Based upon 15 percent compound annual yield with all dividends and/or interest reinvested.

percent. Over a 20- to 30-year period a steady 15 percent compounds your original investment many times, as Table 10–1 shows.

RESISTING THE "HERD INSTINCT"

Nobody likes to walk alone on Wall Street. Investors both large and small have a deep psychological need to buy and sell *en masse*. When the market starts moving up, nobody wants to miss the ship, so everybody jumps on board. But if the ship moves into choppy waters, everyone grabs a life jacket and jumps overboard. The result? Most people have an unsatisfactory voyage. They get on board for the wrong reason and they abandon ship at the first sign of storm clouds.

You should never buy a stock until you have written a list of the reasons you think it represents value and have listed the circumstances and profit level at which you would sell. If you try to make money by playing "follow the leader," you'll probably find yourself at the end of the line. If you buy and sell on the basis of "herd instinct," you're reacting to something that has already happened, so you usually make the wrong move. The Rothschilds built their global banking empire on a simple contrarian investment strategy, "We always tried to be accommodating. When people wanted to buy, we sold. When people wanted to sell, we bought."

PATIENT BUYERS AND SELLERS

When winners go shopping on Wall Street, they buy selectively. They have the patience to keep their money in their pocket until they find an investment that meets the criteria outlined in their game plan.

In a bull market, it usually takes a lot more homework to find stock at a price that still represents value. In a bear market, shrewd long-term investors have an exceptional buying opportunity provided they shop selectively.

Once winners put a good stock in their portfolio, they give it time to mature. This strategy is particularly important in real estate where it takes time to increase cash flow and dividends through property upgrades, releasing, or new acquisitions.

Wise investors don't expect their stock to take off like a rocket. Most investors erroneously expect "instant gratification" in their investments. One investor who bought a high-quality equity REIT recommended by Karel McClellan called her later in the week to complain, "I've owned it three days now and nothing's happened yet." If you want lots of action in just a couple of hours, go to Atlantic City or Las Vegas—not Wall Street.

PROFIT FROM MISTAKES

Nobody wins *all* the time on Wall Street—or anywhere else in life. Statistically, it is virtually impossible. When you do lose, try to learn from the experience. Successful investors always learn from their mistakes and go to great lengths not to repeat them, which is how they refine their investment skills.

If you take a loss, sit down for a few minutes and figure out what went wrong. Jot your thoughts down on paper and tuck them into your investment file. Review them occasionally. For example, did you pay too much? Sell too soon? Buy a stock with poor underlying assets or bad management? Was the company undercapitalized? Overfinanced? Put that information to work for your benefit when you make your next investment.

HOW CAN YOU WIN ON WALL STREET?

The best way to win on Wall Street is with carefully calculated moves coupled with a strong sense of discipline. To do that, incorporate the following four rules into your investment program:

1. **Do your homework.** Don't jump into an investment because your friends or relatives do, or buy something because your broker thinks it is a good deal. Before you make an investment decision, get as much information as possible about the stock or partnership. READ IT. Ask questions.

    Do a little soul searching. Do you understand the investment? Does it make sense to you? Are you psychologically comfortable with it? If not, don't invest.

2. **Use common sense.** Most people don't. The French philosopher Flaubert put it best when he said, "Common sense is not so common."

    Most people have good instincts but don't follow them. The lure of quick profit makes normally level-headed people susceptible to absurd sales pitches. When you're offered a super high return on a no-risk investment, there's usually a catch.

    Likewise, if someone tries to tell you 2 + 2 = 6, tell him or her to go fly a kite. Don't be intimidated by a sales agent's aura of professional knowledge. It is very possible you are facing a good actor with great sales skills, but not much else.

3. **Take responsibility for your money.** When your portfolio is small, you'll need to focus on it yourself, because the really top investment advisors cannot afford to manage small accounts.

    A $5000 to $10,000 portfolio may sound sizable to you, but investment advisors are compensated based on a percentage of assets under management, with their fees ranging from 2 to 3 percent per year. On a $5000 account, that's $100 to $150 per year, which is why the top advisors have minimum portfolio requirements that range from $150,000 to $250,000.

Don't let that discourage you. Managing your money isn't as hard as you might think. In fact, once you get started, you'll discover it can be both challenging and rewarding. In addition to this book, there are many good basic investment books available in any major book store, and magazines like *Money*, *Personal Investor*, and *Sylvia Porter's Personal Finance* bring you sound investment advice each month on a variety of useful topics from real estate to general investments.

4. **Learn to make tough decisions.** There is no room for emotion or ego when you're managing money—it's a bottom line business. You must be able to make buy and sell decisions based solely on facts and figures.

The toughest decision any investor has to make is when to sell a winner—especially if it is still a quality stock. It hurts to let go of a thoroughbred, but it may be the only way to take a profit. And a paper profit isn't really a profit until you put it in your pocket—as many investors found out on Black Monday 1987.

To help you put the decision-making process into perspective, we share how author McClellan (a small investor herself) successfully tackled a series of tough decisions on one stock:

In June 1982, I bought State Street Boston Bank. I was in the market for a good regional bank stock and State Street ranked number 1 on *Fortune*'s analysis of banks. I paid $42.50 for a stock with a 3 percent annual dividend—a very dear price. I swallowed hard when I placed the order. I swallowed even harder when the stock immediately fell to $32—a 25 percent decline. Although the prevailing wisdom is to automatically cut your losses and sell any stock on a 25 percent drop, I didn't.

A careful reexamination of the numbers and the bank's overall plans convinced me the quality I bought was still there. I decided to hang on. Three years later I sold the stock for a 150 percent profit. Annual dividends of 3 percent brought my total return to 156 percent—an average annualized yield of 53 percent.

Finally, I took my profit. The Federal deficit was growing. There were signs interest rates would rise. Although I was now more bullish on the bank than ever, I cashed in my chips.

After I sold the stock it split two for one. Five months later, with a fairly positive near-term economic outlook on the horizon, I bought the stock again, paying $21.50 per share.

By September 1987, I had a 53 percent profit (plus 3 percent in dividends) for an 11-month total return of 56 percent. Despite my continued enthusiasm for the stock, I decided again to sell. The storm clouds were returning and the weather looked even worse this time. The problem of the United States' "twin deficits" was sending a severe warning to investors that a market downturn was coming. So, I took my profit.

When State Street Bank plunged to $18 on "Black Monday," I was glad to have my profit carefully tucked away in T-Bills. But all I could really think of was, "Is the market low enough to buy State Street again?"

Or, as Benjamin Disraeli said, "The secret of success is constancy to purpose."

11

How To Position Yourself for Profit

You've got to know where you're going ... otherwise you won't know it when you get there!

Anonymous

Why do you want to invest? It may be a simple question; nevertheless, many people find it a hard one to answer. Some people have a reflex response: They want to get rich! Others are more specific: they want to make money to buy that Mercedes or the condo at the beach. Finally, there are those who want to plan for retirement—to have money that will insure their standard of living for their twilight years.

Setting investment goals—your overall objective—is important because it will determine, among other things, how much money you need to set aside and what kind of yield you'll have to earn to hit your target.

Before you can set any goals you need to consider three personal requirements:

1.   How much do you need in current income?

2.　How much time do you have to achieve your overall goal?

3.　Is the money involved a one-time amount or will you be able to add to your portfolio on any sort of regular basis?

You should be thinking of these three considerations (they really are constraints) as you develop your investment objectives.

SETTING INVESTMENT GOALS

Basically, the primary objective of any investment is to achieve a return—something that compensates you for the risk involved in the investment. Return comes in either or both of two forms: *income* (interest or dividends) and *appreciation* (an increase in market price). The specific and personal question for you to answer is: What is a good return? What should I aim for—high income or high capital appreciation? Or maybe a combination of both?

The answer depends on factors that you must consider carefully: How much safety do you want? What target have you set for the growth of your investment? Essentially, the questions to be answered before you can set a meaningful objective that will work for you relate to:

Safety

Income

Growth

Liquidity

Safety—How Much Risk?

Safety is a pleasing word and a worthy objective in investing. Here the focus is on keeping the investment secure, or free from loss. Safety is absence of risk. The usual example is: You invest $10,000 in stock. If your investment goes to $9,000 you have a loss. Clear enough. But consider the more subtle difference that occurs when you invest $10,000 in a stock and in three years the stock moves up 35 percent. Not bad, you say. However, suppose in that same period inflation had increased 30 percent. Now that 35 percent increase isn't much in comparison to the erosion of the buying power of your dollar. In three years you have netted (in real dollars) only 5 percent—hardly a good investment. This risk is what is called purchasing power risk. It says essentially that your investment must at least keep ahead of inflation or else you're losing in terms of what those dollars can buy.

Another major risk that all investments are subject to is interest rate risk. As you may have observed, when interest rates go up, stock prices usually go down. The decline is based on two factors: First, increased interest rates mean high corporate costs that cannot be quickly passed on to the consumer, resulting in lower profits. Further, rising interest rates tend to slow consumer spending, reducing corporate profits. In addition, rising rates make other investments more competitive with stock prices, usually at a lower risk. So, people sell stocks and go into money market funds or short-term bonds. The result: lower and lower stock prices. Rising rates also affect bond prices, pushing them down.

A third risk in buying stocks is the business risk. When you buy a stock, you are buying part of the company. If it does well because of good management and market position, you do well. If it doesn't, you're in trouble.

A final risk is market risk. This comes about by just being in the stock or bond market. If the market goes up, usually most stocks go up and vice versa. In an up market where optimism is high, even a mediocre company will usually do well. In a down market, where market psychology is negative, your stock, no matter how good the earnings or management, will usually go down. Incidentally, there is no way to avoid this type of risk except to stay out of the market. Market risk is something you are exposed to no matter how good your stock selection. It comes with the territory!

INCOME

Investors usually achieve their rewards through either income or capital appreciation, preferably both. Of the two, income is usually the most reliable and consistent. You have to decide how much income you need and whether you need it now or later. For retired individuals a high level of predictable income is generally a priority. For those approaching retirement, income in the near future becomes an important objective. For those in their peak earning years, income is not as important as capital growth. Finally, in a tax sheltered environment or where the individual has a low marginal tax rate, income may become more desirable than growth since the more predictable income can compound relatively free of the tax bite.

LIQUIDITY

This is another important factor to consider in setting your investment objective. Liquidity is classically defined as the ability to turn an investment into cash quickly at current market value. The question is simple: How quickly can you sell the asset? Stocks, REITs, some partnerships, and all mutual funds enjoy a high liquidity. Before you buy an investment with limited liquidity, review your cash reserves. Be sure you have enough liquid assets to meet your anticipated needs.

OBJECTIVES

Changes in income will be reflected in subtle shifts in your investment objectives. The relative importance of such factors as savings, liquidity, current income, and capital appreciation, depends upon such variables as your age, income level, wealth, marital status, number of dependents, and debt level. While each investor is unique, some generalizations about the typical mix of investment objectives over an investor's lifetime are possible. For example, if you are between 25 and 35 years of age, your investment objectives might look like this list:

Capital appreciation	40%
Savings	30%

Liquidity	20%
Current income	10%

In this age group, the investor is just getting started on a career. Current income, while climbing, has not been sufficient to accumulate a reserve to cushion against mistakes. Consequently, safety becomes a significant factor. On the other hand, there is also time for a young investor to allow investments to compound and grow. So the portfolio is heavily weighted toward capital appreciation investments. From 35 to 55, the investor is entering the peak earning years. Now capital appreciation becomes of paramount importance. Some savings reserve has been built, and income is coming in fast with expectations of even greater possibilities ahead. So at approximately age 45, investment objectives shift to this emphasis:

Capital appreciation	70%
Liquidity	10%
Current income	10%
Savings	10%

Growth in assets is now needed to pay for the children's college education and to begin initial planning for retirement.

The pattern is clear-cut: in your 30s, 40s, and up to your mid-50s, you should invest more aggressively to get those higher gains. Liquidity should be a secondary consideration.

As you reach retirement at age 65, the mix of investment objectives shifts one final time as follows:

Current income	50%
Savings	30%
Liquidity	10%
Capital appreciation	10%

Appreciation now becomes a lower priority. Sufficient income from safe and secure investment is the paramount consideration.

Although we don't eliminate capital appreciation entirely, since it is a desirable objective in every portfolio, we reduce its role to reflect the retiree's need for higher current income.

In summary, as you move through life from youth to middle age to retirement, your asset mix should reflect changes in current and expected income. A perfect investment fit in your 30s may be too restrictive in your 50s, and too aggressive in your 70s.

Accordingly we have used the general guidelines regarding income, safety, liquidity, and appreciation outlined previously and produced some model portfolios for your consideration. But first, a general comment on portfolios.

MODEL PORTFOLIOS

Investment portfolios are very much like business suits: They should be made to fit their owners, tailored to the individual's needs and objectives and the risks the investor is willing to take to achieve those objectives. Current and prospective earning power and the discipline to save is one factor in determining what risks an individual should take. Age is another factor. Time allows one to compound income effectively. Finally, there is the most important but least quantifiable factor: psychological makeup. In short, what is your risk tolerance level? Can you cope with adversity—specifically, losing money? Can you sleep soundly if your money is at risk? Successful investors learn their psychological limits early and always buy investments they can live with.

Accordingly, with the qualification that a portfolio is specific and personal and that individuals (and couples) may have widely different goals that will require unique solutions, the following section proposes four model portfolios. At least one of these should be suitable as a model for you.

Model Portfolio I

This portfolio is designed for a single person, 35 years of age and younger with the following:

Earnings up to $30,000 a year

Initial investment amount: $15,000

Additional savings: $3,000

Asset Category	Dollar Amount	Percent
Money Market Fund	$2,000	13%
Aggressive Growth Mutual Fund	4,000	27
Emerging Growth Mutual Fund	3,000	20
Real Estate Securities—REITs, Partnerships, Real Estate Mutual Funds	6,000	40
Total	$15,000	100%

Note: Where earnings are above $30,000 and higher, simply apply the indicated percentage to the total amount.

The money market category usually ranges between 10 and 15 percent of a total portfolio and represents a cash reserve with "instant" availability. It also acts as an opportunity pool, allowing you to acquire a new investment you like without having to sell something else. Once used, however, this reserve should be replenished as rapidly as possible. The growth mutual fund selected should be one that is aggressive, meaning higher risk (and hopefully much higher rewards) with little dividend income expected. In addition to an aggressive growth fund, a mutual fund investing in smaller companies or emerging growth companies (fast moving companies in their early stages of earnings gains) is recommended. A representative listing of funds in these categories can be found in Appendix I.

Finally the real estate segment should focus on professionally managed equity investments such as REITs, limited partnerships, and/or mutual funds. With the limited capital available, it is difficult to diversify by buying several individual companies. Also, at this stage of the investment game, the focus should be on the real estate's appreciation potential with only minimal consideration to dividends or income. The real estate securities total of $6000 would include $2000 in an IRA.

Finally, each year the additional savings of $3000 would be distributed equally among three sectors: the aggressive growth mutual fund, the emerging growth fund, and real estate securities. In this case, $1000 would be added to each category every year.

Model Portfolio II

This portfolio is designed for a couple between 36 and 55 years of age with the following characteristics:

Combined income:	$75,000
Initial investment:	$40,000
Additional savings:	$7,500 annually

Asset Category	Dollar Amount	Percent
Money Market Fund	$7,500	18.75%
Growth & Income Stocks	8,500	21.25
Growth Stocks	8,000	20.00
Real Estate Stocks & Partnerships	16,000	40.00
Total	$40,000	100.00%

Note: We have added an asset category of stocks or mutual funds, combining growth and income. This would include stocks where dividend yields are above average (4 percent-plus) with earnings-per-share growth possibilities. Examples would include oil stocks, and electric and telephone utilities, and mutual funds with a primary objective of growth and income a secondary consideration. Mutual funds in this category would be labeled growth and income funds or total return funds. A list of such funds with a history of above average investment performance is given in Appendix I. The real estate segment of the portfolio should be in REIT stocks or real estate-oriented stocks and partnerships. Since we are seeking capital growth, moderately leveraged real estate investments are acceptable. (A moderate level of leverage would be 60 percent.) Also included are convertible debentures and/or convertible preferred stocks. Any additional savings would be distributed equally among growth and income stocks and real estate stocks and partnerships, the rationale for this being that at this stage of life and asset accumulation, the goal is to have some growth but mainly to concentrate on the compounding of growth and income.

Model Portfolio III

This portfolio is structured for a couple between 56 and 65 with:

Combined income	$85,000
Initial investment	$85,000
Additional savings	$18,000 annually

Asset Category	Dollar Amount	Percent
Money Market Fund	$8,500	10%
Growth Stocks	21,250	25
Bond-Mutual Funds—medium to high quality	21,250	25
Real Estate Stocks & Partnerships focus on equity REITs	34,000	40
Total	$85,000	100%

The combined income of our couple is only slightly higher than that of Portfolio II (age bracket of 36–55). It is assumed at this point, however, that there are no longer two wage earners and the single wage earner's salary has peaked as he or she edges closer to retirement. Salary stabilization is more than offset by the reduction of cash drain on gross income for education, dental bills, clothing, and so on. By now, usually, the sons and daughters are educated and out of the nest, and disposable income takes a big jump. Accordingly, our investment focus continues to have a growth orientation, but the percentage of that total is reduced as our ability to take risks declines. One final point: in the money market mutual fund or bond mutual funds category, bonds can be either taxable or nontaxable depending on the investor's situation.

Model Portfolio IV

Our final portfolio is designed for a couple over 65 years of age. Here the combined income and the amount to invest may vary so dramatically on an individual basis that it would be impractical to use dollar amounts. Accordingly, we suggest the following percentages:

Asset Category	Percent
Money Market Fund	20%
Bond Mutual Funds—high quality	40
Real Estate Stocks & Partnerships	40
Total	100%

In the money market fund area we have raised the percentage to 20 percent and we strongly urge that one be selected that invests in only the highest quality short-term obligations, such as U.S. Government paper. Our quality focus is similar in our bond fund concentration. Further, note that we are now up to 40 percent in our bond funds, which brings fixed income to 60 percent of the total portfolio.

Real estate stocks and partnerships account for 40 percent and here our recommendations in distributing that 40 percent are very specific:

Income REITs with *relatively low leverage*	60%
Real estate mutual fund or partnerships with low or no leverage	40
Total	100%

In the final analysis, positioning yourself for profit begins with a sound game plan that provides enough flexibility to meet your changing needs and allows you to capitalize on new investment opportunities. Equally important, positioning yourself for profit requires discipline. You must stick to your game plan and make decisions based on facts, not emotions. Stay the course and you will ultimately be a winner.

Appendix A

Real Estate Investment Trusts

American Health Properties   NY-AHE
9665 Wilshire Boulevard—Ste. 600
Beverly Hills, CA 90210
213-276-6245

American Realty Trust   AS-ARB
(Affil, Southmark Corp.)
1601 LBJ Freeway
Dallas, TX 75234
214-241-8787

Americana Hotels & Realty Corp.   NY-AHR
535 Boylston
Boston, MA 02116
617-247-3358

BankAmerica Realty Investors   NY-BRE
555 California Street
San Francisco, CA 94104
415-622-6530

Beverly Investment Properties Inc.   NY-BIP
99 South Oakland Avenue
Pasadena, CA 91109
818-405-0195

Boddie-Noel Restaurant Properties   AS-BNP
1021 Noell Lane
Rocky Mount, NC 27802
919-937-2197

Bradley Real Estate Trust   OC-BRLYS
250 Boylston Street
Boston, MA 02116
617-421-0675

BRT Realty Trust   AS-BRT
60 Cutter Mill Road
Great Neck, NY 11021
516-466-3100

Burnham Pacific Properties   AS-BPP
1555 Sixth Avenue
San Diego, CA 92101
714-236-1555

Burnham American Properties   AS-BAP
1555 Sixth Avenue
San Diego, CA 92101
714-236-1555

California Jockey Club   AS-CJ
2121 South El Camino Real
San Mateo, CA 94403
415-349-2562

California REIT   NY-CT
601 Montgomery Street
San Francisco, CA 94111
415-433-1805

Cedar Income Fund I   OC-CEDR
CN 5006
Sandusky, OH 44870

Central Realty   OC-CMRT
301 North Ferncreek Avenue
Orlando, FL 32803
305-896-9692

Centrust Trust   OC-CT
830 Post Road East
Westport, CT 06880
203-226-1251

Cenvill Investors Inc.   NY-CVI
Century Village, Adm. Bldg.
West Palm Beach, FL 33417
305-686-2567

Chicago Dock & Canal   OC-DOCKS
401 North Michigan Avenue—Ste. 3145
Chicago, IL 60611
312-467-1870

Clevetrust Realty Investors   OC-CTRIS
Ohio Savings Plaza
Cleveland, OH 44414
216-621-3366

Commonwealth Realty   OC-CRTYZ
3131 Princeton Pike
Lawrenceville, NY 08648
609-896-3344

Consolidated Capital Income Opportunity Trust   OC-CCOTS
2000 Powell Street
Emeryville, CA 94608
415-652-7171

Consolidated Capital Income Trust   OC-CCITS
2000 Powell Street
Emeryville, CA 94608

Consolidated Capital Realty Investors   OC-CCPLS
2000 Powell Street
Emeryville, CA 94608
415-652-7171

Consolidated Capital Special Trust   OC-CCSTS
2000 Powell Street
Emeryville, CA 94608
415-652-7171

Copley Properties, Inc.   AS-COP
535 Boylston Street
Boston, MA 02116
617-578-4900

Countrywide Mortgage   NY-CWM
155 North Lake Avenue Box 7137
Pasadena, CA 91109
818-304-8400

Cousins Properties   OC-COUS
2500 Windy Ridge Pkwy.
Marietta, GA 30067
404-95502200

CRI Insured Mortgage Investments   NY-CII
11300 Rockville Pike
Rockville, MD 20852
301-468-9200

Del-Val Financial   AS-DVL
24 River Road
Bogota, NJ 07603
201-487-1300

Dial REIT   OC-DEAL
11506 Nicholas Street—Ste. 205
Omaha, NB 68154
402-496-7184

Duke Realty-Capital   NY-DRE
8900 Keystone Crossing
Indianapolis, IN 46240
317-848-1100

Eastgroup Properties   AS-EGP
120 North Congress Street
Jackson, MS 39201
601-948-4091

Eastover Corp.   OC-EASTS
120 North Congress Street
Jackson, MS 39201
601-948-4091

Eastpark Realty Trust   OC-ERT
120 North Congress Street
Jackson, MS 39201
601-948-4091

EQK Realty Investors I   NY-EKR
3 Bala Plaza East
Bala Cynwyd, PA 19004
215-667-2300

Federal Realty   NY-FRT
4800 Hampden Lane
Bethesda, MD 20814
301-652-3360

First Continental REIT   OC-FCRES
1360 Post Oak Blvd.
Houston, TX 77056
713-622-2084

First Union Real Estate Equity & Mortgage   NY-FUR
55 Public Square
Cleveland, OH 44113
216-781-4030

Golden Coral Realty Corp.   OC-GCRA
5151 Glenwood Avenue
Raleigh, NC 27612
919-781-9310

Grubb & Ellis REIT   OC-GRIT
One Montgomery Street
San Francisco, CA 94104
415-781-4748

Guild Mortgage Investments Inc. AS-GUM
9160 Gramercy Drive
San Diego, CA 92123
619-590-7711

Harris-Teter Properties AS-HTP
7500 East Independence Blvd.
Charlotte, NC 28212
704-567-3000

Health Care Property Investors, Inc. NY-HCP
3200 Park Center Drive
Costa Mesa, CA 92626
714-751-0989

Health Care REIT, Inc. AS-HCN
One Sea Gate
Box 1475
Toledo, OH 43603
419-247-2800

Healthvest AS-HVT
9737 Great Hille Trail
Austin, TX 78759
512-346-4300

Health & Rehabilitation Properties Trust NY-HRP
215 First Street
Cambridge, MA 02142
617-661-3112

HMG Property Investors AS-HMG
2701 South Bayshore Drive
Coconut Grove, FL 33133
305-854-6803

Hollywood Park Realty Enterprises, Inc. OC-HTRFZ
611 West Sixth Street
Los Angeles, CA 90017
213-627-8145

Hotel Investors Trust NY-HOT
21031 Ventura Blvd.
Woodland Hills, CA 91364
818-883-9510

HRE Properties NY-HRE
530 Fifth Avenue
New York, NY 10026
212-642-4800

ICM Property Investors, Inc. NY-ICM
600 Third Avenue
New York, NY 10016
212-986-5640

International Income Property   AS-IIP
100 Park Avenue
New York, NY 10017
212-972-4080

Investors Mortgage Services   OC-INVG
(Subs. First Financial Savings Assoc.)
1405 North San Fernando Blvd.
Burbank, CA 91504
818-841-8044

IRT Property Company   NY-IRT
200 Galleria Pkwy., N.W.
Atlanta, GA 30339
404-955-4406

JMB Realty Trust   OC-JMBRS
875 North Michigan Avenue
Chicago, IL 60611
312-440-4800

Johnstown/Consolidated Realty   NY-JCT
2000 Powell Street
Emeryville, CA 94608
415-652-7171

L & N Housing Corporation   NY-LBC
2001 Bryan Tower
Dallas, TX 75201
214-746-7111

Landsing Institutional Properties Trust V   OC-LANVS
800 El Camino Real
Menlo Park, CA 94025
415-321-7100

Landsing Institutional Properties Trust VI   OC-LNVIS
800 El Camino Real
Menlo Park, CA 94025
415-321-7100

Lincoln N.C. Realty Fund, Inc.   AS-LRF
21600 Oxnard Street
Woodland Hills, CA 91367
818-704-1590

Linpro Specified Properties   AS-LPO
900 East Eighth Avenue
King of Prussia, PA 19406
215-265-5700

Lomas Mortgage Corporation   NY-LMC
2001 Bryan Tower
Dallas, TX 75201
214-746-7111

Lomas & Nettleton Mortgage Investors   NY-LOM
2001 Bryan Tower
Dallas, TX 75201
214-746-7111

MDC Asset Investors   NY-MIR
3600 South Yosemite Street—Ste. 900
Denver, CO 80237
303-773-1100

Medical Property Investors   AS-MPP
16633 Ventura Boulevard
Encino, CA 91436
818-902-2270

Meditrust   NY-MT
15-A Walnut Street
Wellesley, MA 02181
617-446-6900

Mellon Participating Mortgage   OC-MPMTS
Commercial Property Series 85/10
551 Madison Avenue
New York, NY 10022
212-702-4040

Merry Lane & Investment Company, Inc.   OC-MERY
P. O. Box 1417
Augusta, GA 30903
404-722-6756

MONY Real Estate Investors   NY-MYM
1740 Broadway
New York, NY 10019
212-586-6716

Mortgage Growth Investors   AS-MTG
One Post Office Square
Boston, MA 02109
617-423-4747

MSA Realty Group   AS-SSS
115 West Washington Street
Indianapolis, IN 46204
317-263-7030

Mortgage & Realty Trust   NY-MRT
8360 Old York Road
Elkins Park, PA 19117
215-881-1525

Mortgage Investments Plus, Inc.   AS-MIP
5955 DeSoto Avenue
Woodland Hills, CA 91367
818-715-0311

National Capital Real Estate   OC-NCETS
50 California Street
San Francisco, CA 04111
415-989-2661

New Plan Realty Trust   NY-NPR
1120 Avenue of the Americas
New York, NY 10026
212-869-3000

Nooney Realty Trust   OC-NRTI
7701 Forsyth Blvd.
St. Louis, MO 63105
314-863-7700

One Liberty Properties, Inc.   AS-OLP
515 Madison Avenue
New York, NY 10022
212-935-0931

Paine Webber Residential Realty Inc.   AS-PWM
1285 Avenue of the Americas
New York, NY 10019
212-713-2000

Pennsylvania REIT   AS-PEI
Cedarbrook Hill III
Wyncote, PA 19095
215-927-1700

Pittsburgh & West Virginia Railroads   AS-PW
600 Grant Street
Pittsburgh, PA 15219
212-687-4956

Presidential Realty-A   AS-PDL-A
180 South Broadway
White Plains, NY 10605
914-948-1300

Presidential Realty-B   AS-PDL-B
180 South Broadway
White Plains, NY 10605
914-948-1300

Property Capital   AS-PCT
200 Clarendon Street
Boston, MA 02116
617-536-8600

Property Trust of America   OC-PTRAS
4487 North Mesa
El Paso, TX 69948
915-532-3901

Prudential Realty Trust   NY-PRT
Prudential Plaza
Newark, NJ 07101
201-877-7537

Real Estate Fund Investment Trust   OC-REF
Box 396
Fountain Inn, SC 29644
803-862-3765

REIT of California   NY-RCT
12011 San Vicente Blvd.
Los Angeles, CA 90049
213-476-7793

Realty Refund   NY-RRF
1385 National City Center
Cleveland, OH 44114
216-771-7660

Realty South Investors, Inc.   AS-RSI
1850 Parkway Place
Marietta, GA 30067
404-426-0331

Residential Pension 1   OC-RPSAS
Residential Pension 2   OC-RPSBS
Residential Pension 3   OC-RPSCS
c/o Wilmington Trust Company
Rodney Square North
Wilmington, DE 19890
302-651-1730

Residential Mortgage Investments, Inc.   AS-RMI
2624 West Freeway
Fort Worth, TX 76102

Rockefeller Center Properties, Inc.   NY-RCP
1230 Avenue of the Americas
New York, NY 10020
212-489-4370

Santa Anita Realty Enterprises   NY-SAR
One Wilshire Blvd.
Los Angeles, CA 90017
213-574-7223

Sierra Capital Realty IV   OC-SETD
Sierra Capital Realty VI   AS-SZF
Sierra Capital VI Preferred   AS-SZFPr
Sierra Real Estate EQ83   OC-SETBS
Sierra Real Estate EQ84   OC-SETC
One Maritime Plaza
San Francisco, CA 04111
415-982-4141

Sizeler Property Investors   NY-SIZ
2542 Williams Blvd.
Kenner, LA 70062
504-466-5363

Storage Equities, Inc.   NY-SEQ
P. O. Box 6000
Pasadena, CA 91102
213-682-3601

Strategic Mortgage   NY-STM
700 North Central Avenue
Glendale, CA 91203
818-247-6057

Trammell Crow REIT   NY-TCR
3500 LTV Center
2001 Ross
Dallas, TX 75201
214-979-5100

Travelers REIT   OC-TRATS
99 High Street
Boston, MA 02210
617-338-3460

Travelers Realty, Inc.   OC-TRITS
99 High Street
Boston, MA 02110
617-338-3460

Turner Equity Investors, Inc.   AS-TEQ
10014 North Dale
Mabry Hwy
Tampa, FL 33618
813-963-0768

Universal Health Realty   NY-UHT
367 South Gulph Road
King of Prussia, PA 19406
215-768-3300

USP Real Estate Investment Trust   OC-USPTS
4333 Edgewood Road, N.W.
Cedar Rapids, IA 52499
319-398-8559

United Dominion Realty Trust, Inc.   OC-UDRT
5 East Franklin Street
Box 12365
Richmond, VA 23241
804-780-2691

VMS Hotel Investment   AS-VST
8700 West Bryn Mawr Avenue
Chicago, IL 60631
312-399-8700

Washington Real Estate Investment Trust   AS-WRE
4936 Fairmont Avenue
Bethesda, MD 20815
301-652-4300

Washington Corporation   PSE-TWC
5550 Friendship Blvd.
Chevy Chase, MD 20815
301-657-3640

Webb Investment Property (Del E.)   AS-DWP.A
3800 North Central Avenue
Phoenix, AZ 85012
602-264-8011

Wedgestone Realty   AS-WDG
181 Wells Avenue
Newton, MA 02159
617-965-8330

Weingarten Realty, Inc.   NY-WRI
P. O. Box 94133
Houston, TX 77292
713-868-6361

Wells Fargo Mortgage & Equity Trust   NY-WFM
475 Sansome Street
San Francisco, CA 94111
415-396-3381

Western Investment Real Estate Trust   AS-WIR
3450 California Street
San Francisco, CA 94118
415-929-0211

Appendix Ⓑ

REIT Sampler

The following summaries give you a brief overview of some of the major, publicly traded REITs. For more complete details, write directly to the REIT. The names and addresses of these REITs and others appear in Appendix A, immediately preceding this section.

BANKAMERICA REALTY INVESTORS (NYSE-BRE)

San Francisco-based equity REIT specializing in properties on the West Coast. The portfolio consists of apartments (34 percent), shopping centers (32 percent), warehouse/distribution centers (8 percent), and office buildings (11 percent).

BEVERLY INVESTMENT PROPERTIES (NYSE-BIP)

This Los Angeles-based equity REIT owns 108 nursing homes. In 1987, the trust appointed a new chief operating officer and implemented a strong business plan that should enable the Trust to grow its dividend at 7 percent plus annually into the future.

COUNTRYWIDE MORTGAGE INVESTMENTS (NYSE-CWM)

This new breed of REIT, termed a "CMO REIT," specializes in buying and warehousing residential mortgages to package as collateralized mortgage obligations (CMOs). Collateralized mortgage obligations REITs are interest rate sensitive.

DIAL REIT, INC. (OTC-DEAL)

An Omaha-based equity REIT, Dial owns nine shopping centers in the Midwest. The properties consist of enclosed malls and neighborhood centers anchored by one or more national or regional tenants. Major tenants include J.C. Penney, K-

Mart, Woolworth, Hy-Vu and IGA grocery stores, Herberger's, Shopko, Charming Shoppes, and Cato.

Dial's leases benefit the REIT two ways. First, "triple net leases" protect the REIT from rising costs by making the tenant responsible for reimbursing the REIT for general maintenance, insurance, and real estate tax increases. Second, most leases let the REIT share in the tenant's success at the center by giving the REIT a percentage of gross sales above a predetermined level.

FEDERAL REALTY INVESTMENT TRUST (NYSE-FRT)

A leader in the shopping center industry, Federal's philosophy of upgrading older centers in prime locations has produced steadily increasing dividends and substantial capital appreciation for investors.

Federal's AAA portfolio benefits from superior suburban locations in very affluent neighborhoods adjacent to Washington, D.C. and Philadelphia. Top tenants will pay top dollar to tap these lucrative retail markets. The centers cater to customers with large disposable incomes.

For example, customers line up to pay $37.50 per pound for smoked salmon in Federal's Wildwood Shopping Center (Bethesda, Maryland). Just a few miles away in Rockville, women snap up imported silks in a "discount" fabric store where $39 a yard is a "bargain" and $69 a yard is "less than I'd pay in Paris."

FIRST UNION REAL ESTATE INVESTMENTS (NYSE-FUR)

First Union follows the Rothschild contrarian investment philosophy: "Buy when others are selling. Sell when others are buying. Borrow when rates are low. Lend when rates are high. Be patient when no action is needed."

This strategy has allowed First Union to buy low and sell high. For example, when institutional investors developed an insatiable appetite for downtown office buildings, First Union obliged. They put seven office buildings on the buffet table and walked away with a $65 million capital gain.

The REIT's historical focus has been regional enclosed shopping malls and downtown office buildings. Today the REIT is actively seeking apartment projects to capitalize on the growing demand and shrinking supply of rental housing.

HEALTH CARE PROPERTY INVESTORS, INC. (NYSE-HCP)

An equity REIT specializing in the acquisition and leaseback of nursing homes, rehabilitation centers, psychiatric-care facilities, and medical-office buildings. The REIT's primary focus is nursing homes.

HCP is sponsored by National Medical enterprises, a major health care operator. The REIT follows the recent trend for operating companies in real estate intensive businesses to sell their real estate and maintain the management contract. HCP benefits from National Medical's A-rated credit, expertise in health care, and proven management capability.

HEALTH & REHABILITATION PROPERTIES TRUST (NYSE-HRP)

Based in Cambridge, Massachusetts, HRP invests primarily in income-producing health-care-related real estate. The company's 13 existing facilities emphasize specialized rehabilitation services such as head trauma rehabilitation, pulmonary rehabilitation, substance abuse programs, and adolescent psychiatric programs plus skilled nursing and intermediate care facilities.

Although the company currently has mortgage investments in four properties, future investments will be targeted primarily toward purchase–leaseback transactions on existing health care facilities.

HOTEL INVESTORS (NYSE-HOT)

In 1926, Hotel Investors, a hotel operator, merged with Hotel Properties, Inc., the Los Angeles-based REIT specializing in hotel investments. The combined companies pursue an investment strategy of specializing in the acquisition and renovation of commercially oriented budget hotels in growing U.S. metropolitan markets.

IRT PROPERTY COMPANY (NYSE-IRT)

This Atlanta-based equity REIT invests in shopping centers located in the southeastern United States. In addition to shopping centers (82 percent), the REIT's portfolio includes apartments (10 percent), industrial property (4 percent), and mortgages (4 percent) on properties sold by the REIT.

MEDITRUST (NYSE-MT)

Meditrust is an equity REIT that owns a prime portfolio of subacute health care properties. These include 10 long-term care facilities, one psychiatric hospital, one retirement living center, and two alcohol and substance abuse treatment facilities.

To reduce risk and maximize income, the REIT invests only in existing health care facilities with a proven track record as a quality income-producing investment. All the REIT's properties are leased to the Mediplex Group, Inc., a wholly owned subsidiary of Avon Products, Inc.

MORTGAGE GROWTH INVESTORS (ASE-MTG)

This Boston-based REIT is shifting from mortgage lending to property ownership. Today, MGI meets the standards of an equity REIT with 82 percent of its assets invested in income-producing property. The REIT's goal is to evolve into a pure equity REIT with 100 percent of its assets in property.

NEW PLAN REALTY TRUST (NYSE-NPR)

An equity REIT with an excellent track record for the shrewd acquisition of shopping centers and apartments. The trust buys properties well below their replacement cost; then they upgrade the properties, boosting the quality of tenants and rents in the process.

Geographically, the trust owns 35 shopping centers in eight mid-Altantic and northeastern states plus five apartment complexes in New York, Delaware, and Florida. The trust also has a small industrial building in Princeton, New Jersey.

UNITED DOMINION REALTY TRUST (OTC-UDRT)

An equity REIT that specialized in middle-income apartment projects and—to a lesser degree—shopping centers. The trust's investment approach concentrates on the purchase of properties that can increase cash flow through capital improvements, tenant upgrading, and more attentive management. Geographically, the trust focuses on properties in Virginia and the Carolinas.

United Dominion Realty Trust has increased cash flow and dividends at compound annual rates of 12 to 18 percent over each of the last five years.

In addition to well located properties and excellent management, the trust should benefit from tax reform. The 1986 Tax Reform Act eliminated most of the incentives to build new rental housing. With apartment construction now at an all-time low, existing apartments should increase in value as demand begins to outstrip supply over the next several years.

WASHINGTON REAL ESTATE INVESTMENT TRUST (ASE-WRE)

High quality equity REIT that owns a nearly debt-free portfolio of AAA properties in the prime Washington, D.C. market. Historically, the trust has the highest return on equity of any publicly traded REIT.

The trust's portfolio consists of shopping centers, apartments, and office buildings. Management's successful approach has been to buy low, upgrade, and release at substantially higher rents.

In addition, the trust reduces risk and maximizes cash flow by avoiding substantial debt. Sixteen of the Trust's 23 properties are owned debt-free. The others have small mortgages (usually assumed on purchase) at moderate interest rates ranging from 5.5 to 9.25 percent.

The Trust's properties should continue to benefit from their top locations in the hot D.C. market and the superior management of WRIT's seasoned executives and trustees.

WEINGARTEN REALTY, INC. (NYSE-WRI)

A quality equity REIT that builds and develops strip and community shopping centers. Geographically, the REIT concentrates on the Southwest where it owns 106 properties.

Don't worry about the location. This is one company that knows how to do business in the "oil patch." During the past four years, WRI's net cash flow per share from operations has increased at a 26 percent compound growth rate annually.

Founded in 1948, WRI maintains a conservative debt structure. The REIT's debt-to-net appraised value is approximately one-third.

Appendix Ⓒ

Real Estate Companies and Business Trusts

Name	Exchange	Trading Symbol
ABRAMS INDS INC	OC	ABRI
LP-AMER INS MTG 84	OC	AIMAZ
AMER PACESETTER	PF	AECP
LP-AMER RE PARTNERS	NY	ACP
AMERIBANC INV GP	OC	AINVS
AMREP CORP	NY	AXR
ANGELES CORP	AS	ANG
LP-ANGELES FINC PTRS	AS	ANF
LP-ANGELL CARE MLP	NY	ACR
BAY FINCL CORP	NY	BAY
BEI HOLDINGS	OC	BEIH
BRITISH LAND AMER	NY	BLA
LP-BURGER KING INV	NY	BKP
LP-CAL FED INC PTNRS	NY	CFI
CALPROP CORP	AS	CPP
CALTON INC	NY	CN
CASTLE & COOKE	NY	CKE
CENTENNIAL GROUP	AS	CEQ
CENTEX CORP	NY	CTX
CHAMPION ENTRPRS	AS	CHB
CHRISTIANA COS	NY	CST
CITIZENS GROWTH	OC	CITGS
CLAYTON HOMES	NY	CMH
LP-GMNWLTH MTG AM-A	NY	CMA
COMMONWLTH MTG CO	OC	CCMC
CONGRESS ST PROPS	OC	CSTP
CONTL HMS HOLDING	OC	CONH

COUNTRYWIDE CRDIT	NY	CCR
COVINGTON TECH	OC	COVT
LP-CRI INS MTG INV	NY	CRM
DELTONA CORP	NY	DLT
LP-EMERALD HOMES LP	NY	EHP
LP-EQK GRN ACRES LP	NY	EGA
LP-EQUITABLE RE SC	NY	EQM
EQUITECH FNCL GP	NY	EFG
FAIRFIELD COMM	NY	FCI
FARRAGUT MTG CO	OC	FARR
FED NATL MTG	NY	FNM
LP-FINE HMS INTRNTNL	NY	FHI
FIRST CAROLINA	OC	FCAR
FLEETWOOD ENTER	NY	FLE
FOREST CITY-A	AS	FCE.A
FOREST CITY-B	AS	FCE.B
LP-FORUM RET PFD UN	AS	FRL
FPA CORP	AS	FPO
GEMCRAFT INC	OC	GEMH
GENERAL DEVLPMT	NY	GDV
GENERAL HOMES	NY	GHO
LP-GOULD INVTRS LP	AS	GLP
GRUBB & ELLIS	NY	GBE
HALLWOOD GROUP	NY	HWG
HAMMOND CO	OC	THCO
HOMAC INC	OC	HOMC
HOVNANIAN ENTR	AS	HOV
INDIANA FNCL INV	OC	IFII
INTEGRATED RESC	NY	TRE
INTERGROUP CORP	OC	INTG
LP-INTERSTATE GEN CO	AS	IGC
INTL AMER HOMES	OC	HOME
JOHNSTOWN AMER-A	AS	JAC
K&B HOME CORP	NY	KBH
KAUFMAN & BROAD	NY	KB
KNUTSON MTGE CORP	OC	KNMC
KOGER CO	AS	KGR
KOGER PROPS	NY	KOG
LP-LA QUINTA MTR IN	NY	LQP
LANDMARK AMER	AS	LCO
LANDMARK LAND	AS	LML
LEISURE+TECH	AS	LVX
LENNAR CORP	NY	LEN
LEVITT CORP	AS	LVT
LOAN AMER FNCL-B	OC	LAFCVB
LOMAS & NET FINC	NY	LNF
M/I SCHOTNSTN HMS	OC	MIHO
MAJOR REALTY	OC	MAJR
MDC HOLDINGS	NY	MDC
MISSION WEST PR	AS	MSW
NATIONAL ENTRPRS	NY	NEI
NE MORTGAGE CO	AS	NM
LP-NEWHALL INV PROP	NY	NIP

LP-NEWHALL LAND	NY	NHL
LP-NVRYAN L.P.	AS	NVR
OAKWOOD HOMES	NY	OH
ORIOLE HOMES-A	AS	OHC.A
ORIOLE HOMES-B	AS	OHC.B
PARKWAY COMPANY	OC	PKWY
PATTEN CORP	NY	PAT
PERINI INV PFD	AS	PNVPR
PERINI INV PR	AS	PNV
LP-PRIME FINCL PRTNR	AS	PFP
LP-PRIME MTR INNS LP	NY	PMP
PRINCEVILLE DEV	OC	PVDC
PULTE HOME CORP	NY	PHM
PUNTA GORDA	AS	PGA
RADICE CORP	NY	RI
READING CO	OC	RDGC
REALAMERICA CO	OC	RACO
LP-RED LIONS INNS	AS	RED
REDMAN INDUSTRIES	NY	RE
LP-RETIREMNT LIV MTG	OC	RLIVZ
RIDGEWOOD PROPS	OC	RWPI
ROCKWOOD NATL	PS	RNC
ROUSE CO	OC	ROUS
RYLAND GROUP	NY	RYL
SANTA FE SO PAC	NY	SFX
SAUL (BF) REIT	NY	BFS
SCHULT HOMES CORP	OC	SBCO
SECURITY CAPITAL	AS	SCC
LP-SHOPCO LAUREL CTR	AS	LSC
SKYLINE CORP	NY	SKY
SO ATLANTIC FIN	OC	SOAF
SOUTHLAND FINCL	OC	SFIN
SOUTHMARK CORP	NY	SM
LP-SOUTHWEST RLTY	AS	SWL
STARRETT HOUSING	AS	SHO
LP-STD PACIFIC L.P.	NY	SPF
SUNLITE INC	OC	SNLT
SUNSTATES CORP	OC	SUST
TIERCO GP INC	OC	TIER
TOLL BROS	NY	TOL
LP-UDC-UNIVRSL DEV	NY	UDC
UNICORP AMER	AS	UAC
UNION VALLEY CORP	AS	UVC
US CAPITAL CORP	OC	USCC
US HOME CORP	NY	UH
LP-US REALTY PTNRS	OC	USRLZ
US SHELTER CORP	OC	USSS
LP-VMS MORTGAGE INV	OC	VMLPZ
VYQUEST INC	AS	VY
WASHINGTON CORP	PH	TWC.X
WASHINGTON HOME	NY	WHI
WEBB (DEL E) CORP	NY	WBB
WESPAC INVSTR	OC	WESPS

LP-WINTHROP INS MTG   AS   WMI
WRITTER CORP   OC   WRTC
ZIMMER CORP   AS   ZIM

Source: Audit Investments, Inc., 136 Summit Avenue, Montvale, NJ 07645-1720.
Telephone: (201)358-2735

Appendix Ⓓ

Real Estate Related Industries

SOME REPRESENTATIVE COMPANIES

Building Suppliers

Symbol	Company Name
ACK	Armstrong World
AFG	AFG Industries
AGCJY	Asahi Glass
AST	American Standard
BIRD	Bird Inc.
CRT	Certain-Teed
HUG	Hughes Supply
IDL	Ideal Basic Industries
JSTN	Justin Industries
JWC	Jim Walter
LAF	Lafarge Corp.
LCE	Lone Star Industries
MAS	Masco Corp.
MGAN	Morgan Products
OCF	Owens Corning
SHW	Sherwin Williams
SWK	Stanley Works
TXI	Texas Industries
TYL	Tyler Corp.
USG	USG Corp.

Building Supply Retailers

Symbol	Company Name
YICL	Indal Ltd.
HECH	Hechinger's Co.
LOW	Lowes Companies
PCI	Payless Cashways
SBP	Standard Brands Paint
SHB	Scotty's Inc.

Other Real Estate Stocks

Symbol	Company Name
AHR	Americana Hotels
BRE	Bankamerica Rlty.
BRT	BRT Realty Trust
MRT	Mortgage & Realty Trust
MTG	MGI Properties
MYM	Mony Real Est. In.
WFM	Wells Fargo Mortgage
YCFV	Cadillac Fairview

Investment Builders

Symbol	Company Name
FCI	Fairfield Commun.
MESJY	Mitsubishi Estat.
ROUS	Rouse Co.
YATS	Atlantic Shoppng.
YBCD	Bramalea Ltd.
YBD	BCE Development
YCBG	Cambridge Shop.
YTZC	Trizec Corp. Cl. B.

Mortgage Banking Investments

Symbol	Company Name
CII	CRI Mtg. Inv. II
CRM	CRI Ins. Mtg. Inv.
CWM	Countrywide Mortgage
LMC	Lomas Mtge. Corp.
LOM	Lomas & Nett. Mortgage
RMI	Residential Mortgage
STM	Strategic Mortgage

Appendix E

Glossary of Real Estate Limited Partnership Terminology

Before you invest in a limited partnership, you must be given a detailed description of the offering in a document similar to a stock prospectus. In public partnerships, this document is called the Public Offering Statement (POS). Private partnerships issue a Private Placement Memorandum (PPM).

The POS and PPM contain many trade items unfamiliar to most investors. To help you understand those terms, we are including a glossary from *The Stanger Register*. It provides an easy-to-understand definition of terms common to all limited partnerships.

If you receive a POS and PPM with other terms, or you'd like a more detailed description of these terms, consult your securities broker or accountant.

INVESTMENT DESCRIPTION

Type of Property/Loan/Equipment/Services—Nature of the investment.

Construction Stage—*Existing, to be built*, or *under construction* refers to the status of the property to be purchased.

Borrowing—Maximum allowable leverage expressed as percentage of investment in property.

Percent Specified—Percentage of net offering proceeds earmarked for specific investments.

Number of Properties/Loans—Number of properties purchased or loans made based on fully subscribed offering.

Principal Areas of Activity—Location of properties to be purchased.

Estimated Percent of Distributions Sheltered—For REITs only. Estimated percent of cash distributions in the first five years that are exempt from tax (i.e., sheltered through depreciation, amortization and other noncash deductions).

Estimated 1st Year Cash Distributions—Sponsor's estimate of cash distributions during the twelve months following the close of fundraising, expressed as a percentage of your investment.

Annual Appraisals of LP Interests—Indicates whether or not the partnership provides the limited partners with annual reports indicating the current value of interests.

Anticipated Holding Period—Estimated length of time before partnership is liquidated and proceeds distributed to investors.

COSTS AND REVENUES

Total Front-End Costs—The compensation to the general partner and affiliates for reimbursement of organization and offering costs (including commissions) and maximum allowable acquisitions fees and expenses payable to all parties in connection with the purchase of partnership properties or equipment (based on maximum allowable leverage of sponsor estimate) expressed as a percentage of limited partner capital contribution. Estimates of acquisition fees and expenses to third parties are used in the calculation of Stanger's Offering Terms Ranking, when consistent with fees incurred in prior public programs that have completed property acquisitions or lending activities.

Percent In-Property—The total front-end cost percentage subtracted from 100 percent. This is the percent of limited partner capital contribution available for investment and includes working capital reserves up to 5 percent of limited partner capital contributions.

Operational Phase (Fees)—Fees payable to the general partner and affiliates during the property holding period, including share of distributable cash from operations, management fees and property management fees, including subordination provisions.

Liquidation Phase (Fees)—Fees payable to the general partner and affiliates upon sale of property, including incentive fees (share of net proceeds from sale or refinancing), and commissions, including subordination provisions.

GP (Advisor) Minimum Capital Contribution—Capital investment by general partner or advisor in program expressed in dollar amounts or as a percentage of limited partner or shareholder capital contributions.

GENERAL PARTNER

Years in Program Business—Number of years the sponsor has offered programs, private or public.

Total Public LP (Stockholders) Capital Raised—Cumulative amount of limited partner capital contributions in prior public programs.

Number of Properties Bought/Foreclosed—For real estate equity programs only. Cumulative number of individual properties bought and foreclosed in prior public programs.

Number of Loans Made/Defaulted—For mortgage loan programs only. Cumulative number of individual loans made and defaulted in prior programs.

Properties Sold/Appreciation—For real estate equity programs only. **Properties Sold** is the cumulative number of individual properties sold in prior public programs. **Appreciation** is the compound annual increase in property purchase prices for properties sold. The compound annual increase is the rate that equates the present value of property selling prices to property purchase prices over the weighted average holding period. (See definition of Weighted Average Holding Period in "Trade Jargon" section.) Property purchase price includes acquisition fees, soft dollar development costs and acquisition expenses. Selling price includes notes received upon sale at face value of principal.

Loan Repaid—For mortgage loan programs only. **Loans Repaid** is the cumulative number of individual loans repaid in prior public programs.

Partnerships (Trusts) Liquidated/LP (Stockholder) Gain—**Partnerships (Trusts) Liquidated** is the number of individual partnerships or trusts for which all properties have been sold. **LP (Stockholder) Gain** is the weighted average compound annual increase in the value of investor interests for partnerships or trusts liquidated. The compound annual increase is the interest rate that equates the present value of cumulative investor cash distributions (liquidation proceeds plus prior cash distribution) to total capital contributions (initial capital contributions and assessments). The compounding period is based on the weighted average holding period. (See definition of Weighted Average Holding Period in "Trade Jargon" section.) Notes received upon sale are included in net proceeds at face value of principal.

FINANCIAL DATA

Current Quarter Annualized Operating Cash Distribution/Pretax Yield—Cash distribution from operations for the most recent quarter. Yield equals quarterly cash distribution (annualized) divided by Current Price.

Current Quarter Sale/Loan Repayment Distribution—Cash distribution from property sales or repayment of loans or notes receivable for the most recent quarter.

Total Current Quarter Cash Distribution—Total cash distributions from operations, sales, and loan repayments for the most recent quarter.

Percent of Current Quarter Distributions Sheltered—Nontaxable percentage of cash distributions for the most recent quarter.

Estimated 1987 Operating Cash Distributions/Pretax Yield—General partner's estimate of cash distributions from operations for current calendar year. Yield equals estimated annual operating cash distributions divided by Current Price.

Estimated Percent of 1987 Operating Distributions Sheltered—General partner's estimate of nontaxable percentage of estimated annual operating cash distributions for current calendar year.

Current Net Asset Value Per Unit—The sum of the most recent appraised portfolio value (adjusted for property purchases and sales) and other values (sum of net working capital and long-term assets less long-term liabilities) as of the most recent quarter divided by units outstanding.

TRADE JARGON

Acquisition Fees—Total of all fees and commissions paid by any person to any person in connection with selection, purchase, sale, or development of property by the partnership. Such fees may be designated as real estate commissions, loan application and commitment fees, finders fees, development fees, nonrecurring management fees, initial supervisory fees, consulting fees, or fees of a similar nature.

Acquisition Expense—Expenses of acquisitions such as appraisals, attorney's and accountant's closing fees, costs of title reports, transfer and recording taxes, and title insurance.

Commercial Investment—An investment in shopping centers, office buildings and industrial buildings.

Commercial Net Lease Investment—An investment in commercial property occupied by a corporate tenant on a long-term lease with the tenant paying all costs related to the occupancy and use of the property.

Commissions—Fees payable to the general partner upon the sale of property or equipment owned by the partnership. Such fees are based upon gross sales price and may or may not be subject to subordination provisions.

Cumulative Annual Return—A specified cumulative annual return payable to the limited partner based on a noncompounded percentage of his adjusted capital investment.

Distributable Cash From Operations—Difference between partnership's cash from operations and operating cash expenses for the period, which shall be distributed to partners in amounts determined at the discretion of the managing general partner.

Equipment Management Fee—Fees payable to general partner for specific equipment management services paid from gross revenues derived from operation and lease of equipment owned by the partnership.

Greenshoe—General partner's option to increase size of offering by some fixed amount depending upon market demand.

High Leveraged Programs—Programs that plan to borrow 50 percent or more of purchase price to finance acquisition of properties.

Incentive Fee—Fees payable to general partner for managing affairs of the partnership paid in liquidation phase from net proceeds from sale or refinancing of property or equipment owned by the partnership. Such fees are usually subordinated to the return of limited partner's initial capital investment plus a minimum cumulative annual return on invested capital.

LP Return of Capital—Return of 100 percent of limited partner's original capital contribution.

Low Leveraged Programs—Programs that plan to borrow 0 to 50 percent of purchase price to finance acquisition of properties.

Management Fee—Fees payable to the general partner for management and administration of partnership affairs, usually paid from distributable cash from operations.

Proceeds From a Sale or Refinancing—Net cash realized by the partnership from sale or disposition of partnership property, less (a) amounts necessary to pay all expenses related to the transaction; and (b) amounts necessary to retire mortgage debt related to the partnership property. In the case of wraparound mortgages or similar instruments, net cash realized means principal payments received net of principal payments on underlying indebtedness.

Property Management Fee—Fees payable to general partner or affiliates for specific property management services paid from gross revenues derived from operation of properties owned by the partnership.

Residential Investment—Investment in apartment complexes and single and multifamily housing projects.

Subsidized Housing Investment—Investment in any project that utilizes some form of government assistance for operating or financing costs; or investments in projects that benefit from accelerated amortization or depreciation or special tax credits available under the Tax Code for rehabilitation projects.

Unleveraged Programs—Programs that plan to purchase properties for all cash, without mortgage financing.

Unrelated Business Taxable Income (UBTI)—Income subject to tax in tax-exempt accounts (Keogh, Qualified Pension, Profit Sharing, and Stock Bonus Plans and Individual Retirement Accounts). Limited partnerships generate UBTI in Individual Retirement Accounts by actively carrying on a trade or business or by incurring debt in connection with the acquisition or improvement of property. In real estate programs UBTI is commonly generated by buying properties primarily for resale and by placing mortgages on properties.

Weighted Average Holding Period—Length of time each property (or partnership/trust) was held times purchase price for that property (or investor equity for partnerships/trust). Sum of these multiplications is then divided by aggregate property purchase price (or by aggregate investor equity for partnerships/trust). Holding period for properties sold is measured from date of property purchase to property sale date when cash and notes are received. Holding period for partnerships/trusts liquidated is calculated from date of program formation to date of last property sale when cash and notes are received and proceeds are distributed to investors.

Wraparound Mortgage Loan Investment—An investment in junior mortgage loans secured by a second mortgage on a property. The principal amount of the loan includes the remaining unpaid balance of the existing first mortgage.

Source: The Stanger Register, Robert A. Stanger & Co., L.P., 1129 Broad Street, Shrewsbury, NJ 07702-4314. Telephone: 201/389-3600.

Appendix F

Stanger's Risk Rating for Real Estate Limited Partnerships

As we indicated in the beginning of Appendix E, *The Stanger Register* rates limited partnerships for risk. After subjecting each offering to a rigorous analysis, Stanger assigns risk ratings similar to bond ratings (AAA⁺, AAA, AA⁺, AA, A⁺, and BBB).

In reviewing an offering statement, you may find it helpful to concentrate on the four elements Stanger reviews in assessing risk:

Real Estate—Four essential elements determine risk in a real estate investment—type of property, investment description, leverage, and the amount of property specified.

- Type of Property—The earlier in the construction process you invest, the more risk you take. There are three stages in real estate development. First is the construction period—before the property is ready for occupancy. Risks include problems in completing the building, building cost overruns, or construction delays.

  The second risk phase is the so-called rent-up period which occurs after completion of construction but before substantial occupancy. Here you find out whether the property has a good location; whether the rents projected are realistic; whether operating costs can be controlled; whether the project has enough money to see its way through to substantial occupancy; and, finally, whether the right type of property was built.

  The final risk period is the operational period—between completion of rent-up and the ultimate sale of the property. During this period, management has to negotiate with tenants and determine lease terms and rents; decide on repairs and improvements to remain competitive with new construction; and perhaps most importantly, figure out when to sell or refinance the property. Partnerships purchasing "existing properties" will not assume the risks of the development and completion phases and will know the property's operating history. Partnerships purchasing "under

171

construction" or "to be built" properties will have a much higher degree of risk.

- Investment Description—The nature of the property the partnership will acquire (e.g. commercial, residential, hotels, etc.). The risk here relates to the security and characteristics of the property's income stream (i.e., the credit of the tenants and the length and terms of their leases). Commercial net leases where creditworthy corporate tenants pay all operating and maintenance costs and commit to long-term leases will have less risk than hotels, which rerent rooms daily. Between these extremes lie commercial and residential properties, subsidized housing, and mortgage loans.

- Leverage—The proportion of property purchase price financed by borrowing. Highly leveraged properties require larger cash flows to service debt and, therefore, are most risky. However, leverage can increase your return on equity, and interest payments on debt enhance the shelter aspects of the investment since they are deductible.

- Percent Specified—Risk decreases as the partnership specifically identifies the properties it will acquire. The more properties specified, the easier it is to evaluate the potential performance of the investment. Blind pools do not designate any properties to be purchased. This uncertainty increases risk.

Source: The Stanger Register, Robert A. Stanger & Co., L.P., 1129 Broad Street, Shrewsbury, NJ 07702-4314. Telephone: 201/389-3600.

Appendix G

List of Publicly Traded Master Limited Partnerships

MLP Name	Exchange/Symbol
Real Estate Mortgage Loan	
American First Federally Guaranteed Mortgage Fund 2	OTC/AFMBZ
America First Tax Exempt Mortgage Fund	OTC/AFTXZ
America First Tax Exempt Mortgage Fund 2	OTC/ATAXZ
American Insured Mortgage Investors	OTC/AIM84
American Insured Mortgage Investors Series 85	OTC/AIM85
Angeles Finance Partners	AMEX/ANF
CRI Insured Mortgage Investments	NYSE/CRM
Retirement Living Tax-Exempt Mortgage Fund L.P.	OTC/RLIVZ
Summit Tax Exempt Bond Fund L.P.	AMEX/SUA
VMS Mortgage Investors L.P.II	OTC/VMTGZ
VMS Mortgage Investors L.P.	OTC/VMLPZ
Winthrop Insured Mortgages II	AMEX/WMI
Builder/Developer	
Emerald Homes	NYSE/ENP
Interstate General Co. L.P.	AMEX/IGC
NV Ryan	AMEX/NVR
Southwest Realty	AMEX/SWL
Standard Pacific L.P.	NYSE/SPF
UDC-Universal Development L.P.	NYSE/UOC
Universal Medical Buildings L.P.	OTC/UMBIZ

Fast Food/Restaurant

Burger King Investors Master L.P.	NYSE/BKP
Perkins Family Restaurants L.P.	NYSE/PFR
USA Cafes L.P.	AMEX/USF
Winchell's Donut House L.P.	NYSE/WDH

Hotels/Motels

Aircoa Hotel Partners	AMEX/AHT
Allstar Inns L.P.	AMEX/SAI
LaQuinta Motor Inns	NYSE/LQP
Motel 6 L.P.	NYSE/SIX
Pickett Suite Hotel Master L.P.I	OTC/PSHPZ
Prime Motor Inns L.P.	NYSE/PMP
Red Lion Inns	AMEX/RED

Nursing/Retirement

Angell Care Master Limited Partnership	NYSE/ACR
Forum Retirement Partners	AMEX/FRL
National Healthcorp L.P.	AMEX/NHC

Income Properties

Ala Moana Hawaiian Properties	NYSE/ALA
American Real Estate Partners L.P.	NYSE/ACP
Cal Fed Income Partnership L.P.	NYSE/CFI
Gould Investors L.P.	AMEX/GLP
Marina L.P., The	OTC/MRNZV
Newhall Investment Properties	NYSE/NIP
Newhall Land and Farming Co.	NYSE/NHL
Teeco Properties L.P.	OTC/TPLPZ
U. S. Realty Partners	OTC/USRLZ

Shopping Centers

EQK Green Acres L.P.	NYSE/EGA
Equitable Real Estate Shopping Centers	NYSE/EQM
Shopco Laurel Centre	AMEX/LSC

Miscellaneous

Cedar Fair, L.P. (Amusement Park)	NYSE/FUN
Commonwealth Mortgage of America L.P. (Mortgage Services)	NYSE/CMA
FFP Partners L.P. (Convenience Stores/Gas Stations)	AMEX/FFP
Fine Homes International L.P. (Brokerage/Mortgage Services)	NYSE/FHI
Royal Palm Beach Colony L.P. (Unimproved Land)	AMEX/RPB
Sahara Casino Partners L.P. (Hotel/Casino)	NYSE/SAH
Servicemaster L.P. (Property Services)	NYSE/SVM

Source: The Stanger Register, Robert A. Stanger & Co., L.P., 1129 Broad Street, Shrewsbury, NJ 07702-4314. Telephone: 201/389-3600.

Appendix H

Mortgage-Backed Securities (MBS) Funds and Trusts

NO-LOAD FUNDS

Benham Government Income—GNMA
Benham Capital Management
755 Page Mill Road
Palo Alto, CA 94304
(800) 982-6150 (local)
(800) 227-8380 (out-of-state)

Boston Company GNMA Fund
Boston Company Funds Distributor
One Boston Place
Boston, MA 02108
(800) 225-5267 (nationwide)

Dreyfus GNMA Fund
Dreyfus Service Center
666 Old Country Road
Garden City, NY 11530
(718) 895-1206 (local)
(800) 645-6561 (out-of-state)

Federated GNMA Trust
Federated Securities Corporation
Federated Tower
Pittsburgh, PA 15222-3779
(412) 288-1900 (local)
(800) 245-2423 (out-of-state)

Fidelity Ginnie Mae
Fidelity Distributors Corporation
82 Devonshire Street
Boston, MA 02109
(617) 523-1919 (local)
(800) 544-6666 (out-of-state)

Fidelity Mortgage Securities
Fidelity Distributors Corporation
82 Devonshire Street
Boston, MA 02109
(617) 523-1919 (local)
(800) 544-6666

GNMA Income Trust
Reich & Tang
100 Park Avenue
28th Floor
New York, NY 10017
(212) 370-1240 (local)
(800) 221-3079 (out-of-state)

Lexington GNMA Income Fund
Lexington Management Corporation
P. O. Box 1515
Saddle Brook, NJ 07662
(201) 845-7300 (local)
(800) 526-0056 (out-of-state)

T. Rowe Price GNMA Fund
T. Rowe Price Associates
100 East Pratt Street
Baltimore, MD 21202
(301) 547-2308 (local)
(800) 638-5660 (out-of-state)

Rushmore Fund—Ginnie Mae
Rushmore Group
4922 Fairmont Avenue
Bethesda, MD
(301) 657-1500 (local)
(800) 343-3355 (out-of-state)

Scudder Government Mortgage
  Securities
Scudder Fund Distributors
160 Federal Street
2nd Floor
Boston, MA 02110
(617) 439-4640 (local)
(800) 225-2470 (out-of-state)

Vanguard Fixed Income Securities-
  GNMA
Vanguard Group of Investment
  Companies
P. O. Box 2600
Valley Forge, PA 19482
(215) 648-6000 (local)
(800) 662-7447 (out-of-state)

LOAD FUNDS

Alliance Mortgage Securities Income
Alliance Fund Distributors
140 Broadway
New York, NY 10005
(800) 221-5672 (nationwide)

American Capital Federal Mortgage
American Capital Marketing
2800 Post Oak Boulevard
Houston, TX 77056
(713) 993-0500 (local)
(800) 231-3638 (out-of-state)

Delaware Group Government-GNMA
Delaware Distributors
10 Penn Center Plaza
Philadelphia, PA 19103
(215) 988-1333 (local)
(800) 523-4640 (nationwide)

John Hancock U.S. Government
  Guaranteed Mortgage
John Hancock Distributors
P. O. Box 21
Boston, MA 02117
(617) 572-4120 (local)
(800) 225-5291 (out-of-state)

Home Investors Government
  Guaranteed, Inc.
Integrated Asset Management
666 Third Avenue
5th Floor
New York, NY 10017
(212) 551-6700 (local)
(800) 232-1230 (out-of-state)

Mimlic Mortgage Securities Income
  Fund
Mimlic Asset Management
400 North Robert Street
St. Paul, MN 55101
(612) 298-3826 (local)
(800) 362-3141 (out-of-state)

Oppenheimer GNMA Fund
Oppenheimer Investor Services
P. O. Box 300
Denver, CO 80201
(303) 671-3200 (local)
(800) 525-7048 (out-of-state)

Paine Webber Fixed Income—GNMA
Paine Webber
1285 Avenue of the Americas
18th Floor
New York, NY 10019
(212) 437-3800 (local)

Pilgrim GNMA Fund
Pilgrim Group
10100 Santa Monica Boulevard
Suite 2150
Los Angeles, CA 90067
(201) 461-7500 (local)
(800) 526-0475 (out-of-state)

Prudential-Bache GNMA Fund
Prudential-Bache
One Seaport Plaza
Mutual Funds - 25th Floor
New York, NY 10292
(212) 214-1234 (local)
(800) 872-7787 (out-of-state)

Putnam GNMA Plus Trust
Putnam Financial Services
One Post Office Square
Boston, MA 02109
(617) 292-1000 (local)
(800) 225-1581 (out-of-state)

Seligman High Income–Secured
  Mortgage
Seligman Marketing
One Bankers Trust Plaza
New York, NY 10006
(800) 522-6869 (local)
(800) 221-2450 (out-of-state)

Shearson Lehman–Mortgage
  Securities
Shearson Lehman Brothers
American Express Tower
World Financial Center
New York, NY 10285
(212) 321-7155 (local)

Appendix □

Ranking of Mutual Funds in Terms of Above Average Performance Over the Past Three Years

Name	Size*	Telephone (800) Toll-Free
Aggressive Growth-Capital Appreciation		
Constellation Growth	$148.7	231-0803
Dreyfus Leverage	659.2	645-6561
Fidelity Freedom	1,632.6	544-6666
Hartwell Growth	39.7	645-6405
Hartwell Leverage	47.2	645-6405
Neuberger & Berman Manhattan	629.1	237-1413
Putnam Voyager	653.5	225-1581
Shearson Agg. Growth	142.1	—
Twentieth Century Growth	1,669.2	345-2021
Weingarten Equity	349.7	231-0803
Growth		
Fidelity Destiny I	1,620.6	225-5270
Fidelity Magellan	11,914.0	544-6666
IAI Regional	104.6	—
Loomis-Sayles Cap. Dev.	308.3	345-4048
New England Growth	428.3	343-7104
Northeast Inv. Growth	33.9	225-6704
So. Gen. International	114.0	334-2143

*Assets as of Aug. 31, 1987 (in millions)

T. Rowe Price Growth Stock	1,694.7	638-5660
Thomson McKinnon Growth	475.6	628-1237
Twentieth Century Select	3,308.3	345-2021

Total Return (Growth and Income)

Decatur I	1,778.9	523-4640
Dreyfus Conv. Securities	295.0	645-6561
Eaton Vance Total Return Trust	715.1	225-6265
Evergreen Total Return	1,757.9	235-0064
Fidelity Puritan	5,176.6	544-6666
Fidelity Equity–Income	4,477.0	544-6666
Financial Industrial Income	489.9	525-8085
Fundamental Investors	802.7	421-9900
IDS Equity	501.7	328-8300
Investment Co. of America	5,001.2	421-9900
Lord Abbett Affiliated	4,349.6	223-4224
Nationwide Fund	508.3	848-0920
New England Retirement Equity	168.9	343-7104
Oppenheimer Equity Income	807.4	525-7048
Oppenheimer Total Return	314.3	525-7048
Safeco Income	321.7	426-6730
United Income	1,129.7	—
Vanguard High Yield Stock	199.0	662-7447
Vanguard Index Trust	1,124.4	662-7447
Washington Mutual Investors	3,199.5	421-9900

Corporate Bonds—High Yield

Delchester Bond	406.9	523-4640
Eaton Vance High Yield	36.1	225-6265
Fidelity High Income	1,791.2	544-6666
Financial Bond Shares–High Yield	44.6	525-8085
Investment Port.–High Yield	323.8	621-1048
Kemper High Yield	468.1	621-1048

Corporate Bonds—High Grade

Alliance Bond–Monthly Inc.	40.1	221-5672
American Capital Corp.	154.4	847-5636
Axe–Houghton Income	52.4	431-1030
Bond Fund of America	808.1	421-9900
Sigma Income Shares	33.9	441-9490
United Bond	314.3	—

U.S. Government Bonds

AMEX U.S. Gov. Securities	106.3	872-2638
Carnegie Gov. Sec.–Hi. Yld.	49.4	321-2322
John Hancock–U.S. Gov. Sec.	208.0	225-5291
Lord Abbett U.S. Gov. Sec.	710.2	223-4224
Pru-Bache Gov.–Intermediate Term	824.5	872-7787
Value Line U.S. Gov. Sec.	219.4	223-0818

Mortgage-Backed Securities

Alliance Mortgage Sec.	733.7	221-5672
Franklin U.S. Gov. Series	13,786.9	632-2180
Kemper U.S. Gov. Sec.	4,386.3	621-1048
Putnam U.S. Gov. Guar. Sec.	1,262.6	225-1581
Vanguard Fixed Inc.–GNMA	2,236.0	662-7447
Van Kampen Merritt U.S. Gov.	5,096.5	225-2222

High Quality Tax Exempts

DMC Tax-Free Inc.–USA	372.5	523-4640
Kemper Municipal	1,242.3	621-1048
Mutual of Omaha Tax-Free Income	308.1	228-9596
Seligman Tax-Exempt–National	142.1	221-7844
Stein Roe Managed Muni	492.3	338-2550
United Municipal Bond	445.1	—

Appendix J

Money Market Mutual Funds (Over $500 Million in Assets)

FUNDS SPECIALIZING IN U.S. GOVERNMENT PAPER

Fund/Distributor	Total Assets*
Capital Preservation Fund/Benham	1,769
Cash Equivalent Fund–Govt/Kemper	958
CMA Government Securities Fund/MLPF&S	1,929
Dean Witter/Sears U.S. Govt.MM Trust/Dean Witter	537
Dreyfus MM Instruments–Govt.Secs/Dreyfus	793
Fidelity U.S. Government Reserves/Fidelity	857
Fund for Govt Investors/Rushmore	616
Hutton Government Fund/Hutton	1,162
Lazard Freres–Government Fund/Lazard	632
Liberty U.S. Govt Money Market Trust/Federated	1,442
Merrill Lynch Government Fund/ML Boston	1,622
Pacific Horizon–Government MM/Dreyfus	1,293
Shearson Government & Agencies/Shearson	1,834
Summit Cash Reserves Fund/ML Funds	642
Vanguard MM Reserves–Federal/Vanguard	628

Funds—General

Active Assets Money Trust/Dean Witter	2,309
Alliance Capital Reserves/Alliance	1,458
Alex Brown Cash Reserve–Prime/Brown & Sons	830
Cash Accumulation–MM/Thomson	1,880
Cash Equivalent Fund–MM/Kemper	5,501
Cash Management Trust of America/American Funds	718
Cash Reserve Management/Hutton	3,811

*6/30/87 (millions)

CMA Money Fund/MLPF&S	17,819
Command Money Fund/Command	1,382
Current Interest–Money Market/Criterion	735
Daily Cash Accumulation Fund/Centennial	2,533
DBL Cash Fund–Money Market/Drexel	1,436
Dean Witter/Sears Liquid Asset/Dean Witter	6,768
Delaware Cash Reserve/Delaware	981
Dreyfus Liquid Assets/Dreyfus	7,232
Dreyfus MM Instruments–Money Market/Dreyfus	517
Fidelity Cash Reserves/Fidelity	6,547
Fidelity Daily Income Trust/Fidelity	2,801
Fidelity Select–Money/Fidelity	687
Franklin Money Fund/Franklin	1,070
General Money Market Fund/Dreyfus	654
Hutton AMA Cash Fund/Hutton	2,221
IDS Cash Management Fund/IDS	858
ED Jones Daily Passport CashTrust/Jones & Co.	618
Kemper Money Market Fund/Kemper	4,166
Kidder Peabody Premium Account/Kidder	769
Lazard Freres–Cash Management Fund/Lazard	671
Liquid Capital Income Trust/Carnegie	1,238
Mass Cash Management–Prime/Mass Finl	617
Merrill Lynch Institutional Fund/ML Boston	1,235
Merrill Lynch Ready Assets Trust/ML Funds	10,416
Merrill Lynch Retirement Reserves Money/ML Funds	2,987
National Liquid Reserves–Cash/Smith Barney	1,390
New England Cash Mgmt–MM/New England	685
Oppenheimer Money Market Fund/Oppenheimer Inv	611
Pacific Horizon–Money Market/Dreyfus	743
Paine Webber Cashfund/ Paine Webber	4,020
Paine Webber RMA–Money Market/Paine Webber	2,164
Pierpont Money Market/Morgan Stanley	1,142
T. Rowe Price Prime Reserve Fund/Price	3,042
Prudential–Bache Moneymart Assets/Pru–Bache	4,191
Reserve Fund–Primary/Resrv	1,450
Scudder Cash Investment Trust/Scudder	1,141
Shearson Daily Dividend/Shearson	3,688
Shearson FMA Cash Fund/Shearson	1,455
Short Term Income Fund–MM/Reich & Tang	755
SteinRoe Cash Reserves/Stein Roe	798
Tucker Anthony Cash Management/Tucker Anthony	699
Vanguard MM Reserves–Prime/Vanguard	3,063
Webster Cash Reserve Fund/Kidder	1,503

Tax Exempt Money Market Funds

Active Assets Tax-Free Trust/Dean Witter	1,052
Alliance Tax-Exempt Reserves–General/Alliance	810
Calvert Tax-Free Reserves–MM/Calvert	721
CMA Tax-Exempt Fund/MLPF&S	7,733
Command Tax-Free Fund/Command	692
Daily Tax Free Income Fund/Reich & Tang	1,122
DBL Tax-Free Fund–Money Market/Drexel	546
Dean Witter/Sears Tax-Free Daily Income/Dean Witter	954

Dreyfus Tax-Exempt Money Market/Dreyfus	2,921
Federated Tax-Free Trust/Federated	3,586
Fidelity Mass Tax Free Money Market/Fidelity	553
Fidelity Tax-Exempt Money Market/Fidelity	3,823
General Tax Exempt Money Market/Dreyfus	572
Kidder Peabody Tax Exempt MM/Kidder	914
Municipal Cash Reserve Management/Hutton	2,047
Nuveen Tax-Exempt Money Market Fund/Nuveen	1,868
Paine Webber RMA–Tax-Free/Paine Webber	943
Pierpont Tax Exempt MM Fund/Morgan Stanley	1,167
T. Rowe Price Tax-Exempt Money Fund/Price	1,279
Prudential–Bache Tax-Free Money Fund/Pru–Bache	709
Shearson Daily Tax-Free Dividend/Shearson	743
Shearson FMA Municipal Fund/Shearson	1,001
Tax-Exempt Money Market Fund/Kemper	1,716
Tax-Free Instruments Trust/Federated	1,402
Tax-Free Money Fund/Smith Barney	1,112
USAA Tax-Exempt Fund–Money Market/USAA	515
UST Master Tax-Exempt Funds–Short Term/Boston Co.	516
Vanguard Muni Bond–Money Market/Vanguard	1,815

Appendix K

Closed-End Bond and Stock Funds

The following is a listing of investment companies with a portfolio of bonds:

AM Govtlnc
AllstaMuni
AMEV Secs
American Capital Bond Fund
Bunker Hill Income Securities
Circle Income Shares
CNA Income Shares
Colonial Municipal Income Trust
Current Income Shares
Drexel Bond-Debenture Trading Fund
DryStratMun
Excelsior Income Shares
First Australia Prime Income Fund
First Boston Income Fund
Fort Dearborn Income Securities
GlbGvt
Global Yield Fund
Hatteras Income Securities
INA Investment Securities
Independence Square Income Securities
InterCapital Income Securities
John Hancock Income Securities
John Hancock Investors

Kleinwort Benson Australian Income Fund
Lincoln National Direct Placement
Lincoln National Convertible Securities
MFS Government Markets Income Trust
MFSInc&Opp
MFS Multimarket Income Trust
MFS Municipal Income Trust
MMIncInv
Montgomery Street Income Securities
Mutual of Omaha Interest Shares
NYTEI
Nuveen Municipal Value Fund
NuvValCal
NuvValNY
Pacific American Income Shares
PutnmCnv&Bd
State Mutual Securities
Transamerica Income Shares
USLife Income Fund
Vestaur Securities

Closed End Stock Funds

The following is a list of publicly traded closed-end investment trusts with portfolios predominately invested in common stocks, and the exchange on which their shares are traded. The funds are divided into two groups: diversified common stock funds and funds that are "specialized" such as convertibles, equity, and country or area funds such as the France Fund, Italy Fund, and so on.

DIVERSIFIED COMMON STOCK FUNDS

	Stock Exchg.		Stock Exchg.
Adams Express	NYSE	Liberty All-Star	NYSE
Baker Fentress-n	OTC	Niagara Share	NYSE
Blue Chip Value	NYSE	Nicholas App Gr Eq	NYSE
Clemente-Gbl	NYSE	Quest Value Cap	NYSE
Equity Guard	NYSE	Quest Value Inc	NYSE
Gemini II Cap	NYSE	Royce Value	NYSE
Gemini II Inc	NYSE	Schafer Value	NYSE
Gen'l Amer Inv	NYSE	Source Cap	NYSE
GlobalGr Cap	NYSE	Tri-Continental	NYSE
GlobalGr Inc	NYSE	Worldwd Value	NYSE
GSO Trust	NYSE	Zweig Fund	NYSE
Lehman Corp	NYSE		

SPECIALIZED EQUITY AND CONVERTIBLE FUNDS

	Stock Exchg.		Stock Exchg.
Amer Cap Cv	NYSE	Gabelli Equity	NYSE
ASA Ltd	NYSE	Germany Fund	NYSE
Asia Pacific	NYSE	H & Q Health	NYSE
Bancroft CV	AMEX	Helvetia Fd	NYSE
BGR Prec. Mtls	TOR	Hopper Sol	NYSE
CNV	NYSE	Italy Fund	NYSE
CNV Pr	NYSE	Korea Fund	NYSE
Castle	AMEX	Mexico Fund	NYSE
CenFd Canada	AMEX	Mg Sm Cap	NYSE
Cent Sec	AMEX	Petrol & Res	NYSE
Claremont	AMEX	Pilgrim Reg	NYSE
Couns Tandem	NYSE	Prg Inc	NYSE
Cypress Fd	AMEX	Reg Finl/Shs	NYSE
Duff Phelps Utils	NYSE	Scandinavia	AMEX
Ellsworth CV	AMEX	Scudder Ner Asia	NYSE
Emerging Med Tech	AMEX	Taiwan Fund	AMEX
Engex Inc	AMEX	TCW Conv Secur	NYSE
Fin News Comp	NYSE	Templeton E Mkt	AMEX
1st Australia	AMEX	Utd Kingdom Fd	NYSE
First Fin Fund	NYSE	Z-Seven-p	PAC
France Fund	NYSE		

Appendix L

Closed-End Mutual Funds

LIMITED SHARES EQUAL INTERESTING PROFIT POTENTIAL

Closed-end mutual funds are a way to buy—at a price usually below asset value—a broad, diversified list of common stocks. Compare this with the usual mutual fund (open-end) that sells at exactly asset value plus any sales charge!

The closed-end funds have a fixed capitalization; they do not continuously sell shares in themselves—a characteristic that spares them the embarrassment of the heavy redemptions in a stock market decline, but at the same time limits their growth. Another difference between closed-end and open-end funds is that the closed-end funds are traded in auction market—usually the New York Stock Exchange—while the open-end funds—which don't limit the shares they sell—are sold directly. When you buy closed-end shares, you pay regular brokerage commissions on them at rates that are a good deal lower than the usual 4 to 8 percent sales load charged on purchases of open-end load funds.

The mechanism of the marketplace gives rise to the discount. Most closed-end funds have traditionally traded at discount, though a few that specialize in foreign issues (The Korea Fund and the Taiwan Fund, for example) often sell at a premium. The discount (or premium) lies in the spread between the market price of the underlying shares and the pro rata asset value of the securities in the closed-end company's portfolio. For example, in late 1987, the Blue Chip Value Fund was trading at 6-1/8 and its net asset value was $7.26 a share. In 1987 the Royce Value Fund was selling at $7.00 with a net asset value of $8.17 per share, representing a discount of more than 14 percent.

Lehman and Tri-Continental are among the larger funds in the business, and they typify the diversified common stock funds. Their portfolios tend to read like a list of the Fortune 500. Their objective is conservative growth.

Closed-end funds cover a wide range of objectives, concentrating in areas such as gold or oil stocks. In addition, there are a number of other specialized equity companies that focus on countries and their stocks: France Fund, Germany Fund, Helvetia Fund (Switzerland), Italy Fund, and Mexico Fund. In addition there are geographic area funds: Asia Pacific, Scudder New Asia, and the Scandinavian Fund among them. Global High Yield, John Hancock Securities and John Hancock Investors, Mutual of Omaha, and the Transamerica Fund are all bond funds.

Some of these closed-end funds are on the *Forbes* honor roll of the best performing investment companies each year. On the whole, though, most of the big closed-end funds have done no better for their shareholders than the open-end funds. What makes the closed-end funds interesting, is the discount. The spread between the asset value of closed-end funds and their market value is the key to what can be a profitable investing strategy. It all turns on what Thomas J. Herzfeld, one of the few analysts to specialize in the closed-end funds, calls an "excessively large discount." The discount varies from fund to fund. An "excessively large" discount means a deviation of 10 percent or more.

Herzfeld cautions: "If the normal discount is not judged correctly it can work as much against the investor as for him. Also not all funds' net asset values move exactly proportional to the market. Therefore, it is essential for a trader to be familiar with the historical performance and current portfolios of any fund he considers trading."

Current discount figures on the closed-end funds can be found weekly in the *Wall Street Journal*, in the financial pages of the *New York Times* and the weekly *Barron's* (in the mutual fund section). The dividend yield is also listed.

While the discount to market value is critical, other factors include:

Comparison of the quality and liquidity of the fund's portfolio;

A rating of the fund's management performance over the last one, three and five years;

The level of portfolio turnover;

The level of debt, if any, in the capital structure and the volatility of the stock.

These factors, in varying ways, affect the discount at which the fund trades. You can get an idea of the normal discount by constructing a moving average of the discounts on each closed-end fund.

It is hard to isolate the impact such variables as management performance have on the size of the discount at which a fund trades. Theories about the reasons for the cut rates abound. Some argue the discounts are a function of the potential tax liabilities stockholders absorb on unrealized portfolio gains. Another view states that the discount reflects brokers' unwillingness to put any hard sell behind relatively unromantic securities on which commissions are smaller than other load-type mutual funds.

In summary, a closed-end investment company offers a way to buy stocks at a discount. You should therefore keep your eye on the level of the discounts. If they widen, closed-ends may be a good buy. While the discount is important, you should consider such factors as management performance, management fees, and portfolio turnover, too.

Appendix Ⓜ

Investment Terminology

Wall Street talks in jargon—buzz words with their own special meaning. Many of them may be familiar to you. Others, less so. Fortunately, none is very complicated. Even a beginner can pick the terminology up quickly. To help you find your way up and down the street (or through an annual report), we've listed the most useful and commonly used terms.

Accrued Dividends—Dividends that are due but have not been paid yet. Since dividends are dependent upon earnings, they are not a debt of the corporation until directors declare them. With cumulative preferred stock, where the rate is fixed and must be paid before dividends on common stock, any declared but unpaid dividends are accrued.

Accumulation—Quietly purchasing a large position in a single security.

Allotment—When demand for a new issue exceeds the number of shares being issued, the underwriter divides the shares up among preferred customers anxious to buy the new issue. The purchaser's portion of the new issue is his allotment.

Amortization—Reducing the principal of a long-term loan through regular installments that usually include interest.

Arbitrage—Buying a security in one market and selling it in another at a higher price. For example, if French francs are selling for 14 cents on the Paris exchange and 15 cents on the New York foreign exchange, an arbitrageur simultaneously buys francs in Paris and sells them in New York. The profit: 1 cent per franc minus the cost of executing the transaction.

Arrears—An unpaid debt that is due.

At the Market—To buy and sell at prevailing rates. Example: Investor tells his broker to sell the Reliable Real Estate Trust at the best price he can get today.

Balance of Payments—The ratio of money flowing into and out of a country.

Balance of Trade—The monetary difference between a country's imports and exports. It is favorable if exports exceed imports, ominous if imports outweigh exports.

Bid and Offer—The prices at which a buyer will buy (bid) and a seller will sell (offer) a security.

Big Board—Nickname for New York Stock Exchange.

Blind Pool—Funds pooled by investors, often in a limited partnership, to make one or more unspecified investments. The investors must rely upon the sponsors' ability to select a quality asset.

Blue Chip—Common stock in high quality company, usually an industry leader. Company has solid track record of favorable performance under varying market and economic conditions. For this reason, blue chip stocks generally sell at fairly high prices and carry high price–earnings multiples.

Blue Sky Laws—State laws that regulate the sale of securities inside its border.

Boiler Room—Phone bank of high-pressure salesmen hired to lure unsophisticated investors into dubious deals through telephone solicitations. They generally work evenings and weekends calling investors at home.

Bonus Stock—Common stock given to purchasers of preferred stock in new offerings.

Book Value—Cash value of corporation's total assets minus all liabilities. To get the book value per share, divide the difference by the total number of equity shares outstanding.

Call—A contract to buy a security at a fixed price within a specific time period.

Capital Gain or Capital Loss—Profit or loss taken on the sales of securities or real estate.

Capitalization—Total amount of securities issued by a corporation. It includes stock, bonds, and debentures.

Cash Flow—Corporation's earnings after paying dividends and taxes.

Cats and Dogs—Speculative, low grade securities. They cannot be used as collateral to buy on margin.

Certificates of Deposit—Negotiable (cash) instruments sold by banks, savings & loans, and brokerage firms. Maturity dates range from 90 days to 5 years.

Day Order—An order given by an investor to his broker to buy or sell a security. It is good for one day only.

Debenture—Long-term debt secured by assets and general credit of borrower, usually a corporation. In the case of debenture stock, it is a priority stock ranking ahead of preferred and common.

Discount Rate—Interest rate the Federal Reserve charges on loans to member banks. It influences the amount and cost of credit available.

Discretionary Orders—Investor authorizes broker to buy and sell securities using his or her own judgment. This strategy carries greater risk for investors.

Dividend—A portion of earnings paid by a corporation to shareholders as a return on their investment.

Dollar Averaging—Investing a specific amount of money, at regular intervals, in a particular security. For example, an investor bullish on Profitable Properties REIT decides to invest $200 each month (or quarter, or year, etc.) in the stock. Because of price fluctuations, the $200 may buy more stock one time, less stock another time.

Double Taxation—This term refers to corporate dividends because they are taxed once at the corporate level and again at the shareholder level.

Dummy—A director appointed to a corporate board to represent an investor who has a substantial investment in the company. The dummy has no financial investment in the company.

Equity—Stockholder interest in a company, represented by common and preferred stock. If an investor buys on margin, equity is the value of securities in the account minus the debit (loan) balance.

In real estate, equity is the difference between the value of the property and the mortgage (if any) on the property.

Ex-Dividend—When corporate directors declare a dividend, it is usually payable to stockholders of record as of a given date. Shareholders of record on the given date receive the dividend even if they sell their stock before the dividend is actually paid. *After* this date, the stock is quoted "ex-dividend," meaning without dividend.

Fiscal Year—A corporation's accounting year, which may be different from the calendar year. For example, October 1st through September 30th is a fiscal year used by some corporations.

Growth Stocks—Companies with a steady increase in gross earnings. Because of their potential to become an industry leader, they typically pay modest dividends and reinvest the bulk of their earnings into further corporate research and development.

Guaranteed Stock—Stock issued by one corporation whose dividend (and perhaps principal, too) is guaranteed by another corporation. The guarantor corporation usually has a higher credit rating.

Hedge—A form of insurance used by professional traders to minimize losses through possible stock price fluctuations. The trader arranges a purchase or sale of stock to offset possible losses in another stock trading position.

Holding Company—A corporation that owns all or the majority of stock in another operating company (or several other companies).

Hypothecation—To pledge negotiable securities as collateral for the repayment of a loan.

In and Out—Buying and selling a security in a short period of time.

Interim Certificates—Temporary stock ownership certificates issued to buyers of new issues until formal certificates can be printed and issued.

Interim Dividend—A small dividend paid one or more times per year. Usually done in anticipation of a larger dividend at close of corporate tax year.

Leaseback—Most commonly, when a corporation sells (and then leases back) its real estate holdings. This strategy is popular with operating companies who don't want to keep their money tied up in valuable real estate. It is a popular technique with hotel chains, fast-food franchises, nursing home operators, and so on.

Listed Securities—Those securities approved for public trading on a stock exchange. Most are listed daily in major metropolitan newspapers and *The Wall Street Journal.*

Load—A term common to mutual funds and open-end investment companies. It refers to that portion of the purchase price kept by the sponsor to pay sales commissions and distribution costs.

Locked In—An investment where an investor cannot liquidate his position without unpleasant financial consequences. For example, an investor with a substantial capital gain who would incur a sizable tax liability if he sold his stock.

Long—To hold securities in anticipation of a price increase is to be "long" in a stock.

Long Pull—Securities bought with intention of holding them for a long time.

Margin—To purchase securities on a leveraged (debt) basis. The buyer puts up 50 percent of the purchase price and borrows the balance from his broker.

Melon—When a board of directors "cuts a melon" it isn't sacrificing a honeydew. It is declaring a large cash dividend.

Nominee—A corporation trustee or person holding securities for the benefit of the true (undisclosed) owner.

Noncumulative—Preferred stock on which a corporation is not obligated to pay a dividend unless the dividend is earned and declared by the board of directors. For this reason, unpaid dividends do not accrue.

Odd Lot—A stock purchase less than the established trading unit. For example, if a stock trades in units of 100 shares, a purchase of 75 shares is an "odd lot" transaction.

Off-Board—Purchase and sale of unlisted securities.

Option—A contract to buy or sell a specific security at a specific price within a specified time frame.

Paper Profits/Losses—Unrealized gains or losses.

Parent Company—A company that owns enough stock in another company to control it.

Participating Preferred—Preferred stock that enjoys regular dividends plus a percentage of the company's earnings.

Pegging—Manipulating the market by attempting to control the price range of a specific security.

Penny Stocks—Highly speculative, low priced stocks, usually selling under $2 per share.

Preferred Stock—This stock enjoys a superior payment position over common stock. Dividends are always paid first on preferred stock, second on common stock. However, bonds and floating corporate debt rank ahead of preferred stock.

Prospectus—Printed document, usually in booklet form, summarizing the details of a new stock issue or an existing company's expansion plans.

Proxy—A stockholder unable to attend a stockholders' meeting may authorize a third party to vote his shares at the meeting. This is done by giving the third party written authority (a proxy) to attend and vote the shares. Most companies will supply a proxy form for any shareholder unable to attend.

Put—An option to sell a specified number of shares of a specified stock to the option purchaser within a specified time frame.

Pyramiding—Using paper profits on a stock as collateral to buy more stock on margin.

Registered Representative—A licensed securities salesman who works for a brokerage firm. He is authorized to buy and sell stocks for clients of the firm.

Regulation T—Federal regulation that specifies the amount of credit brokers can extend to clients wishing to buy securities on margin. The present limit is 50 percent of the market value of the security.

Rights—A benefit given to existing stockholders to buy additional stock or bonds in the company below the current trading price.

Round Lot—The trading unit established by an exchange, commonly 100 shares. Stocks must be traded in round lots. Trades for other denominations are called odd lots.

Scaling—An investor places stock orders at regular price intervals instead of placing the entire order at once. In theory, this helps him buy or sell at gradual increments instead of larger price swings.

Selling Against the Box—To sell securities you own without actually delivering them. The seller sells "short." He covers his position by buying and delivering the securities, or eventually tendering his existing shares.

Settlement Day—For the buyer, the day he must pay for securities purchased. For the seller, the day he must deliver the securities he sold.

Short Covering—An investor buys back securities he sold but did not own.

Short Sale—An investor sells securities he does not own in the belief their price will drop and he can buy them later at a lower price.

Sleeper—A security thought to be undervalued.

Split Up—A stock split. The existing shares in a company are multiplied by dividing each of the present shares into two or more shares. This reduces the price of each share while preserving the total value of the stock.

Spread—The difference between the bid and offer price of a security. For example, if investors are offering $10 per share for ABC Homebuilders and sellers are asking $11 per share for the stock, the spread is $1.

Thin Market—A market with few offers to buy or sell a security. It could be a factor of supply and demand or it could be caused by a closely held security concentrated in the hands of just a few owners.

Treasury Stock—Issued by a corporation and later repurchased by it. The stock has no voting or dividend rights. Despite the name "Treasury," this stock has nothing to do with securities issued by the U.S. Treasury.

Twin—A completed securities transaction; the purchase and sale of a stock.

Underwriting—The underwriting agent or agents guarantee the sale of a securities issue at a stated price—even if they have to purchase part of the issue themselves.

Unlisted Securities—Those not listed on any organized exchange.

Warrant—The right to buy a particular stock at a specific price. A warrant is merely a "right to buy"; it does not entitle the holder to any dividends and is not backed by the corporation's assets. Warrants may be perpetual or for a specific period of time (usually quite long).

Wash Sales—Stock transactions that look like a sale. In reality, there is no real change in ownership because the investor sells the stock in one account and buys it back in another. Wash sales are forbidden on all the exchanges.

Working Capital—Difference between a corporation's total current assets and liabilities.

Yield—The rate of return currently being paid in the form of dividends on a security. It is expressed as a percentage of the trading price. For example, a stock trading at $10 per share with total annual dividends of 75 cents is yielding 7.5 percent.

Appendix N

Sources of Information and Bibliography

The following is a summary of the types of information (including statistical data) that you may find useful in your investment planning. Included are periodicals, company information sources, newsletters, investor software, and books recommended for careful reading.

PERIODICALS—Daily, weekly, bi-monthly and monthly publications:

- *Wall Street Journal*
  200 Liberty Street
  New York, NY 10281

- *New York Times*
  229 W. 43rd Street
  New York, NY 10036

- *Investors Daily*
  P.O. Box 25970
  Los Angeles, CA 90025
  Packed with valuable data for the detail oriented investor who likes lots of statistics-volume-price relationships. Supplements the *Wall Street Journal*.

- *Barron's* (weekly)
  200 Burnett Road
  Chicopee, MA 01021

- *Business Week* (weekly)
  1221 Avenue of the Americas
  New York, NY 10020

- *Forbes* Magazine (Bi-monthly)
  Forbes Subscriber Service
  60 Fifth Avenue
  New York, NY 10011
  The annual mutual fund survey which is published in August is particularly useful.

COMPANY INFORMATION

Three major investment advisory services are available at your local library or stockbroker's office. These can also be purchased: *Moody's, Standard & Poor's* and *Value Line*.

Moody's Manuals are a basic source of historical data, bound in large and complete volumes published annually for most industrial, utility, transportation, and finance companies.

Standard & Poor's publishes a series called *Standard Stock Reports* covering those stocks listed on the New York and American Stock Exchanges and the over-the-counter markets. Each stock is summarized on a single sheet that includes a description of the company, a chart of the company's performance, and detailed statistical data. Standard & Poor's also publishes a smaller and useful *Stock Guide*—a monthly handbook with one-line summaries of more than 5000 common and preferred stocks.

Value Line is a service that produces a concise one-page summary of individual company statistics and prospects. More than 1500 companies are covered. The service is available at most libraries or through:

Value Line Investment Survey
Arnold Bernhard & Company, Inc.
711 Third Avenue
New York, N.Y. 10017

In addition, specific company information can be obtained from the following:

Securities & Exchange Commission Reports

These may be obtained from either the Commission or sometimes directly from the company. The most important reports are the 8K, the 10K and the 100. However, for basic analysis, only the 10K is really needed. A detailed compilation of company operations, the 10K usually is much more specific than the company's annual report. If requested, 10K reports are frequently available from the reporting company.

Financial and Investment Newsletters

There are now more than 1000 financial newsletters published in the United States. Some focus on mutual funds exclusively and others center on particular kinds of stocks. Nearly all are geared to give buy, sell, and hold recommendations to investors who use those tips to determine their own trades. The investors who profit most from a newsletter are those with the time and interest to be independent and who make their own trades through a discount broker.

You often pay for research you never use when you get investment advice from both a newsletter and a full-service broker. However, if you are happy with your broker and his or her research material, you might consider the right newsletter as a potential enhancement to your investment batting average.

Finding the right newsletter is no easy task, though a good starting point would be a newsletter about newsletters. *Hulbert Financial Digest* rates the performance of 100 investment newsletters.

Some newsletters, like *The Chartist* and *The Professional Tape Reader*, are strictly technical services that select stocks on the basis of their price, volume, and the patterns that these factors create. Other newsletters concentrate on balance sheet, income or statistical data such as earnings or the economic outlook of an industry. *Value Line* focuses on the health and prospects of specific companies. Some newsletters select stocks of a particular type, such as *Growth Stock Outlook* or *High Technology Investments*.

It is almost impossible to determine which newsletters consistently yield the best returns to investors, and it is possible to find good advice from a variety of methods. One criterion that can be used to eliminate choices is cost. Newsletter services can range from $49 to $500 a year, and there appears to be no correlation between high prices and high returns!

Mutual fund investors can use newsletters effectively too. *O'Malley's Fidelity Watch*, for example, tracks the many mutual funds offered by Fidelity investments. Incidentally, this weekly letter is not affiliated with Fidelity. Another newsletter is the *Mutual Fund Forecaster*, which gives monthly buy, sell, and hold recommendations, with risk ratings for mutual funds.

Following is a sampling of some of the newsletters that could be of use to you. All are worth considering to see if they fit your particular investment needs.

The Astute Investor (Robert J. Nurock)
P.O. Box 988
Paoli, PA 19301

Audit Realty Stock Review
Audit Investments
136 Summit Avenue, Suite 200
Montvale, NJ 07645

Daily Graphs (William O'Neil)
Box 24933
Los Angeles, CA 90024

Donoghue's Moneyletter
Box 540
Holliston, MA 01746

Lynn Elgert Report (Lynn Elgert)
P.O. Box 1283
Grand Island, NE 68802

Emerging Growth Stocks
7412 Calumet Avenue
Hammond, IN 46323

Kenneth J. Gerbino Investment Letter (Ken Gerbino)
9595 Wilshire Blvd. Suite 200
Beverly Hills, CA 90212

Growth Stock Outlook (Charles Allmon)
P.O. Box 15381
Chevy Chase, MD 20815

The Hume MoneyLetter
10866 Wilshire Blvd. Suite 200
Los Angeles, CA 90024

The Outlook (Arnold Kaufman)
Standard & Poor's Co.
25 Broadway
New York, NY 10004

The Professional Tape Reader (Stan Weinstein)
P.O. Box 2407
Hollywood, FL 33022

The Prudent Speculator (Al Frank)
P.O. Box 1767
Santa Monica, CA 90406

Telephone Switch Newsletter (Richard J. Fabian)
P.O. Box 2538
Huntington Beach, CA 92647

Value Line New Issue Service
711 Third Avenue
New York, NY 10017

Value Line OTC Special Situations Services
711 Third Avenue
New York, NY 10017

Volume Reversal Survey
211 South Clark Street
Box 1546
Chicago, IL 60690

Wall Street Digest (Donald H. Rowe)
101 Carnegie Center
Princeton, NJ 08540

The Zweig Forecast (Dr. Martin E. Zweig)
P.O. Box 5345
New York, NY 10150

Investor Software

Value Line Software
711 Third Avenue
New York, NY 10017

Value Line's software for personal computer use has stock selection mode (screens data base of over 1600 stocks), portfolio management, and spread sheet files.

Dow Jones News/Retrieval Service
P.O. Box 186
Drexel Hill, PA 19026-9973

For use with your personal computer, the Dow Jones News/Retrieval gives you:

Exclusive online access to the full text of the *Wall Street Journal*

Current and historical stock quotes

Business news as it happens

10K and 10Q data

Leading investment analysts' reports

Complete corporate profiles

Books

All books listed below can be obtained from your local library or by purchase from your book store.

The New Game on Wall Street
by Robert Sobel
John Wiley & Sons (1987)

Once Wall Street meant just stocks and bonds. Today, the investment game is also played with options, futures, index options, junks, and zero coupons. Wall Street authority Robert Sobel explains the cataclysmic changes that have stood the equity, debt, and money markets on their heads—and what these changes mean to investors. Sobel puts it all in perspective and helps you use this knowledge to sift through your alternatives, develop a winning strategy, and put it into action.

The Intelligent Investor (4th revised edition)
by Benjamin Graham
Harper & Row (1986)

This book, a classic of its kind, teaches the principles of sound investing through value-oriented stock selection. It employs long-term investment strategies and contains rich insights. The late Benjamin Graham was one of the most respected investment authorities of the past 50 years.

The Battle for Investment Survival
by Gerald M. Loeb
Simon & Schuster (1957)

Gerald Loeb was a successful stockbroker who made millions practicing what he preached; to wit: Let the stock market guide your investments. One of his basic tenets was never, ever average down on a stock . . . but *do* average up. Most investors do the reverse.

The Battle for Stock Market Profits
by Gerald M. Loeb
Simon & Schuster (1971)

A follow-up to the best seller *The Battle for Investment Survival*—worth reading for Loeb's further thoughts.

Investment Policy
by Charles D. Ellis
Dow Jones-Irwin (1979)

Charles Ellis is managing partner of Greenwich Associates, a financial consulting firm. In this book he reviews what investment strategies work for successful investments. He points out "the overwhelming evidence shows that market timing is not an effective way to increase returns for one dour but compelling reason: on average and over time, it does not work."

Finally, Mr. Ellis refers to an unpublished study of 100 large pension funds. In their experience with market timing, the research team found that, while all the funds had engaged in at least some market timing, not one of the funds had improved its rate of return as a result of its efforts at timing.

How To Buy Stocks
by Louis Engel and Peter Wyckoff
Little, Brown & Co. (1976)

One of the better stock primers even though it is dated. It presents all basic information in a clear, easy-to-read style.

How to Make Money in Wall Street
by Louis Rukeyser
Doubleday (1974)

A witty and useful overview of how the stock market works and what makes its practitioners—the analysts, stockbrokers and portfolio managers—tick. Rukeyser's decades of reporting on the financial scene, including hosting the television program "Wall $treet Week With Louis Rukeyser," have produced a perspective that is both informative and engaging for all investors.

Investment Analysis and Portfolio Management
by Cohen, Zinbarg and Zeikel
Richard D. Irwin, Publisher (5th Edition) (1986)

An authoritative college-level textbook on the investment process. It is detailed and somewhat tedious, but close to the last word on the subject and, through recent editions, up-to-date.

Stock Market Primer (revised edition)
by Claude N. Rosenberg, Jr.
Warner Books, 1987

For the ABCs of buying and selling stock, Rosenberg's book is a goldmine of information for new and experienced investors. In addition to the basics, Rosenberg discusses possible strategies and explains why stocks behave in predictable cycles. Chock full of useful lists and tables.

Security Analysis of Stock Trends
by Benjamin Graham
McGraw-Hill (1962)

Somewhat dated but quite simply the bible of investing for the value-oriented analysis. It is difficult reading but well worth the effort.

Understanding the Economy—For Those People Who Can't Stand Economics
by Alfred L. Malabre, Jr.
Dodd, Mead and Company (1975)

A primer on how our economy works by a *Wall Street Journal* staffer.

The Only Other Investment Guide You'll Ever Need
by Andrew Tobias
Simon & Schuster (1987)

Humor, ridicule, and exaggeration point out that the hoary maxim applies well to the whole spectrum of "get-rich-quick" deals: There's no such thing as a free lunch! Entertaining book.

Index